The Inner Path
A Guide to Living a More Mindful, Fulfilling, and Spiritual Life

Geoff Bell-Devaney, M.Ed.

Inner World Publishing
Copyright © 2021 by Geoff Bell-Devaney

Printed in the United States of America

First edition printing: 2012
First revised edition printing: 2014
Second revised edition printing: 2021

ISBN-13: 978-0692223147

ISBN-10: 0692223142

Front cover original artwork by Geoff Bell-Devaney

www.geoffbell-devaney.com

Also by Geoff Bell-Devaney:

A Mindful Approach To Parenting: Insights on Raising Our Children With Wisdom, Awareness, and Acceptance

For those who seek the truth.

Table of Contents

Introduction

The Inner Path
A Guide to Living a More Mindful, Fulfilling, and Spiritual Life

Geoff Bell-Devaney, M.Ed.

Introduction

I began experiencing debilitating panic attacks shortly after celebrating my thirtieth birthday. Some present... Here I was, young, healthy, and apparently going insane. My mind was racing, my stress level was through the roof, and my future was quickly imploding. All systems were on red alert from an invasion that appeared to be coming from somewhere inside of me. I had absolutely no idea what was happening. I'd never had a panic attack before much less experience them on a daily basis. I was beyond confused. I seriously thought that I might have been losing my mind or something. And, in some beautiful way, I eventually did. Nonetheless, at the time, I quickly began feeling profoundly helpless, scared, and alone.

Before the panic attacks started I was living a pretty good life. Five years earlier, I had graduated from one of the top business schools in Canada and then lived and worked in a number of places like Japan, Whistler, and the Caribbean; exploring life and the world and pursuing my passions at the time of surfing, skiing, snowboarding and off-road motorcycle riding. I was young and seemingly invincible and trying to have as much fun and excitement as possible. My life was one big adventure. Just a few months before the panic attacks started, I'd spent the whole summer down in Baja surfing with friends before driving back up to Whistler to start a new job at a heli-skiing company. My future was looking bright. But now, suddenly everything was rapidly changing. Seemingly out of the blue, my life was being turned upside down. These panic attacks were starting to put a serious cramp in my lifestyle. How could I keep exploring, playing, and having fun if I couldn't even sit in a restaurant without totally sweating bullets?

It didn't help, I suppose, that from the beginning, I hadn't told anyone what I was experiencing. Ultimately, I didn't want to admit to myself or anybody else how much I was hurting and how much constant pain I was in. I was suffering alone, in silence. Looking back now, I was in complete denial of my emotions – the masculine dilemma personified, I suppose. I didn't want to acknowledge my pain or let other people know what I was feeling because that would have meant on some level that all of these new uncomfortable feelings were, in fact, actually part of my experience. That they were real. And if they were real, then there was probably a really good chance that they were always going to stick around because after they had first shown up, they hadn't gone anywhere. And if they weren't going anywhere, then that would likely mean that I would probably always be in pain and never get my old life back... So naturally I didn't want to tell anyone about them. I just wanted them to go away. (Can you see where I was coming from here?...) I figured that if I could just tough it out and ignore my reality, that things would eventually get better, that everything would go back to normal. That didn't happen, however. Everything started to get progressively worse and my reality soon became much more difficult to ignore...

The frequency and intensity of the panic attacks quickly increased and I soon had to quit my job and leave Whistler. When that happened, it became clear to me how someone in my position with nowhere else to turn could easily end up on the street, homeless and lost. Forgotten. Fortunately, I was able to stay with various family members, and while I was extremely grateful that I had somewhere to go, the last thing I wanted to do at thirty years old and having lived all over the world was move back in with my parents. Staying with my sister for a while in a cool, little town in the Rockies was one thing, but my parents? That most definitely hadn't been a planned extended stop on my world tour.

It quickly became apparent that these panic attacks were clearly not going away no matter how hard I tried to ignore them. I started to become concerned that these uncomfortable feelings were actually going to stick around forever and that this nightmare was going to become my permanent reality. I feared that things were never going to get better, only worse. Nonetheless, I still didn't let anybody know what was happening to me. I had so many questions with seemingly no answers and kept them all to myself. What was actually going on inside of me? Would things ever get better? And what if they didn't? Where was I going to end up then? What would ultimately become of me?

It wasn't until quite some time later that I would find out. It wasn't until I had lived this hell for a year and a half and couldn't live it any longer that things started to become clear. It wasn't until then that I realized I had indeed received a birthday present. A present that I had never asked for and at the time most certainly didn't want – a present that would end up profoundly changing my life.

You see, one day I realized that I was running out of gas. My ability to persevere in the face of such an intense and constant challenge was rapidly fading. I could no longer continue battling the ever-present panic attacks and my profoundly stressed-out existence. I had reached the lowest point of my life and felt utterly hopeless and alone. I was in constant, intense pain and couldn't find my way out of it. I was beyond despondent. In that moment, it became abundantly clear to me how someone could decide to end their life.

I didn't want to even consider that option, however, and vowed to keep fighting as best I could. I didn't want things to end up like this, but had no idea what to do. All I could think of was to try to somehow improve my self-confidence (which I now see as an admittedly heroic, but ultimately misguided attempt to simply cover up my pain), so I went out and purchased a half-dozen books that I thought might be helpful. The first one I read mentioned the concept of surrendering to a higher power, which was something that I had absolutely no interest in even considering. I didn't want to give up. I wanted to overcome this - to beat it, not give in to it, not surrender. Plus, I had no desire whatsoever to believe in any God or religion or power greater than myself. Yet, I was utterly lost and afraid. I was in so much pain and my will to keep fighting it was almost gone. So with tears in my eyes and believing in nothing but my desperate and desolate future and not knowing what else to do, I dropped to my knees and repeated a phrase that I had read in that new book: "Thy Will, not mine."

And then it happened. The panic attacks suddenly stopped and a deep calmness came over me. I was, after a year and a half of absolute misery, suddenly at peace. Total peace. And just like in the song "Amazing Grace", I could, for the first time, see. I was no longer blind. I was awake. It was as if the painful shell of unconsciousness - of ignorance - that I had been unknowingly living in up to that point had instantly broken apart and fallen away and I had been freed from my suffering. And in some profoundly new way, everything suddenly made complete sense. I could now see that my whole life, including the intense pain and confusion that I had been experiencing over the past year and a half, had been perfectly designed to bring me to that very moment - to that moment of awakening. I was also able to see that there was a whole world inside of me just waiting to be explored and understood – a world of truth, insight, and emotion. And since that moment, I have been doing my best to search for the truth; for the truth about myself and life. I have been investigating my inner world and growing in insight. And I have been exploring and learning from my emotions.

I can now clearly see how important it is to acknowledge and embrace all of our emotions, for if we don't, we are missing out on one of the most beautiful and vital parts of life, as well as the key to a truly meaningful one. And that is something I couldn't understand before my awakening. Back then, when I was overcome with challenging emotions, all I could do was let them drag me deeper into suffering. But after my awakening, as the stillness I had been experiencing started to fade and more emotions once again came back into my life – at times, very intensely – I began to more clearly understand how paying attention to their lessons could allow me to grow in insight and awareness. How my emotions could enable me to become more real and empowered. And I was also able to see, most importantly, how they could help me remember and realize - with greater depth and duration the longer I have continued on this inner path – the peace and presence I first experienced at the moment of my awakening; the oneness with life, with my true self - with the present moment.

Before my awakening, I didn't realize the importance of my emotions. I was basically just living the typical unconscious human existence of constantly avoiding my uncomfortable emotions and chasing those that felt good, as so many of us inherently do. I didn't know that our emotions are an infinite source of wisdom and the path to a life of greater happiness and inner peace. In fact, I didn't know anything about my emotions. I was emotionally unaware. I was emotionally unintelligent. Until that point, my life had been all about the physical - doing things like pushing my limits in a variety of extreme sports, and the intellectual – studying endlessly to score at the top of my university classes when I needed to and tenaciously spending several years learning to speak Japanese even though it was something that by no means came naturally to me. Despite having an abundance of both the physical and the intellectual in my life, what was missing, I came to realize, was the emotional. By not having any connection to my emotions, I had no true connection to myself, to others or to life.

I can now clearly see that life runs much more smoothly when we have all three elements – the physical, the intellectual, and especially the emotional - in place. When we are not engaged in the physical realm, we can lose our fluidity, our balance, and our sense of play. When we aren't stimulating ourselves intellectually, we can become stagnant, incurious, and set in our ways. And most importantly, when we aren't connected to our emotions, we can't know the truth. When we aren't in touch with our emotions, we are alone. We can't see that life is supporting us in every moment; that it is constantly guiding us, teaching us, and helping us heal. When we aren't in touch with our emotions, we are willful and lost and unable to comprehend our inherent spirituality, our inherent divinity. When we start to acknowledge and embrace our emotions, however, we can begin growing in self-awareness. We can begin to know ourselves.

And that is ultimately what this book is about. It is about knowing ourselves. It is about acknowledging all of the different parts of us and all of our experiences. It is about discovering our deepest truths and our deepest fears. It is about letting life in, so that it can let us in. So that it can teach us. So that we can become more insightful, empowered, and connected to a deeper source of authentic creativity.

The first time I experienced this deeper form of creativity was while writing this book. At the time, I was doing Julia Cameron's course The Artist's Way. One morning, I was writing in my journal as the course entailed and asking the universe what I should do with my life when suddenly words began moving through me that were not my own, but at the same time were very familiar to me. Every day over the course of the next few weeks, I sat down to do my morning journaling and had the exact same experience. And each time I did my best to get out of the way and simply write down the words that were coming through me without influencing them in any way possible. Remembering nothing at all of what I had written each day, when I read the collection of my journal entries as a whole from start to finish, I realized, much to my surprise, that they comprised a complete book; one describing the path - the inner path - to a more mindful, fulfilling, and spiritual life.

In hindsight, I believe that all of the insights I had garnered since my awakening opened the doorways for this book to come through me, to be heard and expressed by me. I believe that when we listen deep inside we can hear our innermost truths. And the words in this book are my innermost truths. I didn't so much write this book as live it.

As we begin listening to our own innermost truths, we can start knowing ourselves. We can begin seeing our lives with greater clarity and compassion. It is my hope that this book can help you do that. That it can help you more clearly know yourself and be able to more confidently navigate your inner world, so that you can discover all of the wisdom, peace, and happiness that can be found there.

As we start investigating our lives, we will begin learning from them. We will begin growing in awareness and insight. We will heal. As we embrace and explore our inner world, we will start experiencing deeper presence and greater equanimity. As we begin to more fully know ourselves, we will start to live a more authentic, empowered, and fulfilling life. We will start to realize our true potential. And we will begin to remember who we truly are beyond our hopes and our dreams, our successes and our failures. We will begin to know ourselves beyond our names and our narratives, our fears and our frustrations.

We will begin to remember who we truly are. We will start to awaken.

We will start to awaken to our true peace and our true power.

To our true purpose and our true self - to the present moment.

To life.

To love.

<u>1</u>

<u>The Power of Our Emotions</u>

We often lose ourselves in a search for pleasure - for fulfillment of the senses, letting them be our guide.

Instead, we must learn to dive deeper than the field of sensation and begin listening to our body's inner wisdom.

We must constantly ask ourselves "what do I feel?" and start investigating our inner world for reasons why we might be experiencing something.

As we begin touching our own hearts, our own aliveness, by staying open to our emotions, we will discover a life that is more rich and alive in every moment.

*

Our inner compass is constantly pointing us toward a greater realization of who we are and who we are meant to be. Although outside circumstances may lead us to believe otherwise, our inner truths will never lead us astray. They will show us the path through the darkest storms and the brightest skies.

We can learn to let these truths guide us throughout the day. We can allow these truths to lead us through the subtle lies and deceptions of life; the lies and deceptions that we allow others to tell us, and that, most importantly, we tell to ourselves.

*

We can find connection to the truth and to the world around us through our emotions. By beginning to trust and learn from them, we can begin swimming effortlessly with the current of life - with the current of our own life - and not against it.

As we begin embracing our inner reality, we will find our energy flowing and our spirits brightening. Life will become more alive and we will grow in wisdom and inner peace.

*

No one else can tell us how we feel. Only we have this information. We should use it wisely and often and grow into ourselves with each breath and step that we take. Our emotions, as we begin paying attention to them, will provide us with greater clarity and understanding about our lives. As we start acknowledging their presence and opening to their wisdom, we will begin to see how we might live a more truthful, heartfelt existence in every moment and discover a compassion born of an acceptance of how things are, rather than how we might want them to be.

*

All of life is waiting for us to swim with it, to play in its peaceful waters. We no longer have to swim alone in a sea of sadness, loneliness and regret. We simply have to accept whatever we are feeling in this and every moment. We just have to watch our emotions as they pass by within us, within our awareness. We just have to feel them. As we begin doing this, we will start to truly feel alive and will begin flowing in harmony with the currents that are around us and within us.

2

Understanding Our Patterns

If we are not aware of our emotions or the patterns in our lives, we will likely continue to react to life in the same old unconscious ways that we always have. When these patterns were first forming, we were perhaps only children, reacting to some fear or unmet need within us. At that time, we may have behaved in a myriad of ways - by withdrawing or lashing out, for example - strategies designed to protect us from the outside world and the perceived dangers it held.

Unfortunately, at that time, we may also have been unable to accept and integrate the powerful emotions we were feeling, and now, as adults, are still affected by these same wounds, our lives constantly influenced by their hidden presence. Ruled to some degree by the past, we are never truly in the present. Not trusting life or the wisdom of the emotions within us, we live separate from ourselves and from others.

And yet, it is entirely possible to begin learning from our emotions and patterns and start responding to life - to interact with it, instead of simply hiding from it or pushing it away. To do this, we just have to begin embracing the present moment and those feelings and sensations that we have, for so long, chosen to avoid. So the next time you find yourself becoming uncomfortable in a difficult situation and want to react in ways that might cause you or another person pain, remember that there can be another way.

*

The first step you can take to begin responding to life and freeing yourself from your old, dysfunctional patterns is to simply bring your attention to your body as it begins the process of reacting. Silently become aware of the tightening and the speeding up inside. Patiently watch the resistance and discomfort grow. Do your best to just take note of any thoughts that arise and keep in mind that it is easy to become debilitated by over-thinking yourself into a state of despair.

Simply observe yourself and try to understand what is happening. Notice how your old pattern is trying to trap you and how you are reacting to it, and remember that you can respond to any situation from a place of greater balance and clarity. It just takes practice to be able to do this. Over time you will begin to feel more comfortable responding in this way.

*

So that we can better see how our unconscious reactions to our emotions can leave us in patterns that are not always in our best interest, we should also do our best to figure out why we are doing something. There are many more internal forces and motivators at work than we are aware of, so we should be careful not to make decisions until we have considered all of the reasons behind our

5

choices. Hasty decisions often lead to unnecessary discomfort in the future.

As we question why we are doing something, we should look to see what emotional factors might be motivating our decision. Is it from an old fear that we are running or hiding? Are we feeling small, scared, and alone and not wanting to acknowledge it? Are we running from the imagined pain in this or a future moment?

Rather than just blindly putting ourselves into a situation, we should instead first run to ourselves. We should check in and ask, "How will this serve me?" and "How will it hurt me?" Remember, we are very precious beings and are always being supported by life. We should always try to look for ways that feel right and follow them.

We also have to understand that these feelings are often hiding behind a fear of change. It is important to respect when we are feeling scared and to understand that this is a natural reaction to growing and moving in new directions. And again, we have to remember to run to ourselves. We must do our best to hold and accept our fear within our awareness and listen to our spirit calling from behind the voice of fear – to the wise man or woman inside who is urging us on, through our fear.

*

To change our unhealthy patterns, we have to begin listening inside and growing from our experiences, from our successes and our mistakes. And we have to work with our lives as they are, as we find them in each moment, for that is ultimately all that we can do. We can practice constantly checking in with ourselves to see how we are feeling and ponder the answers that we hear rising up from the wealth of truth that we are. By doing this, we can begin learning from every situation and let our inner truths help us determine how best to make changes in our lives.

*

Until we are able to face ourselves, our patterns, and our fears, life will continue to give us the same lessons over and over. In order to learn from them and move beyond them, we have to remain dedicated to changing and growing despite any outside forces that may make us want to remain small and hidden. We must keep pushing forward, gently, within ourselves. Even when we are around people that we imagine make it difficult for us to change, we have to be firm in our commitment to realizing our potential.

The societal pressures that are influencing us can take many forms and be very strong. To overcome them, we must commit to embracing change and to better understanding ourselves. We must not let others' perceptions of who we are and who we might become limit us from growing and changing our patterns. This is a dangerous roadblock, for it is often very subtle and stems from a lifetime of living in fear and seeking approval.

*

We must be a light unto ourselves and do our best to not let others' limited behaviors keep us limited.

We have to grow. We must change.

It is the natural way of life.

3

Living in the Now

We should do our best to avoid wanting things to be different than they are in this moment, and try to accept whatever we are experiencing without judgment or frustration.

Pulling away from what is results in pulling away from ourselves and from the reality of life.

*

Whenever there is pain, there is an opportunity for learning - for growing and becoming more whole.

However, in our moments of discomfort we often try to change our reality by resisting what is. We try to make our "now" more enjoyable, and in the process, often fail to see the deeper meaning of our experiences.

*

We might instead try to stay open to life as we find it in every moment and realize that we cannot always have things our way; that we are not in charge. By doing this, we can begin to accept life as it is, even if it is not how we want it to be. We can learn to be grateful for each moment and accept how it makes us feel inside. And we can practice watching our feelings to see if they will change. The winds of emotion will surely blow again and before we know it, a new one will be drifting by. And we can do our best to find the patience to let it come, and to let it pass. We can try to accept what is. This will help us accept what was and what will be.

*

To live more fully in each moment, we have to begin watching our inner world and start accepting the various thoughts and feelings that we are experiencing without judgment.

*

We should also be kind toward ourselves no matter what we feel, and not run from our emotions, for if we do, we will only be running from ourselves. Instead, we should run to ourselves in every moment.

*

As we are able to live more easily in each moment by practicing being mindful, our days will become more stimulating and beautiful. It is as if we were to spend one full hour savoring the smell and taste of a single cup of tea. That tea, like any other experience, will become much richer if we are able to be totally present to all of the sensations that we find.

10

When we are open to life and the abundance of each moment, our experiences become more alive. It is a bit like the first time we share a kiss with someone - we move into a state of now so deep and pure that we often remember those wonderful moments for as long as we live. It can almost be like this with a cup of tea (but without the nervousness, of course!)

*

It is important to remember to always try to gently pull ourselves back into this moment. This is something that takes practice, like learning a new sport or language. Staying grounded in our bodies and doing our best to feel our emotions and sensations can help us to do this. With careful repetition and loving attention we can become more used to living in the now. And as we do, we will discover that the present moment is typically very peaceful and also very full.

*

We ultimately do not need anything in this moment. Even if we are running out of air, we do not need anything. Of course, we do need air to live, but ultimately we are much more than this body that our spirit inhabits. A very practiced individual who was able to live fully in the now would accept this dire situation with the curiosity of a child at a museum.

But make no mistake. This does not mean that we are to act passively. We are not meant to simply stand idle if we have another choice. We should always look for solutions and ways to better any situation, to improve our lives and those around us. The individual mentioned above, upon realizing that her air supply was diminishing, would do everything in her power to replenish it. This would be a good example of self-love and self-preservation.

We are not meant to stand by helplessly while life takes the wind from our sails. Like a sailor on the high seas, we should always be checking the wind's direction and be prepared to make appropriate adjustments.

But if we do find ourselves becalmed, there is no point in fussing, hoping, or praying. The wind will come up when it is ready to do so. In the meantime, we can reach for a paddle or simply enjoy the calm for it will surely change. Even the driest deserts in Africa get their rains, and jumping, dancing, and praying for the heavens to open up won't make any difference. We cannot make a lion into a tiger no matter how hard we try.

*

Rather than resisting reality, we should do our best to accept every moment exactly as it is and understand that it is absolutely perfect for us at this particular stage of our life. The more that we can embrace all of our emotions and experiences, the more we will be able to understand this.

4

The Power of Forgiveness

We should do our best to not blame other people for what we are feeling. We should try to be grateful for their presence in our lives. The people who make us the most uncomfortable are often the best teachers we will ever have. We should always wish them well. This is an excellent way of remaining empowered and unaffected by their words and actions. We can overcome the unpleasantness of their behaviors by extending our heart to them, no matter what they may have done to us. This pushes out hate and helps open the possibility of inner and outer peace.

*

When we are feeling angry at someone or sad at how they may have hurt us, we might try summoning the courage to wish them happiness and peace. We are all capable of giving love and this is an excellent way of practicing this. And when we can invite others to receive peace and goodness, it allows us to be more open to it as well. As we do this, we will begin to see our resentment and frustration fade away and start to understand the power of forgiveness.

This is the path of the heart. This is the path back to yourself and the power that you thought you had lost so long ago. This is the way back to the person that you thought you could never be.

That you always wanted to be.

That you forgot you were.

*

Never be afraid to extend peaceful thoughts to those who you think have wronged you, for these people are not unlike you. Who among us hasn't done something that has hurt another? Like all of us, these people are often acting in ways in which they are unaware, blinded to the reality of fairness, equality, and truth. They, too, are moving toward greater self-realization and acceptance. At heart, we are all the same.

*

We are all still like children at times, acting in ways that reflect some early fear or unmet need. Try to recognize this child within yourself and imagine the effects of these hidden fears on your own actions and have compassion for the ways in which you have acted out of fear, sadness, or anger as a result.

Consider a painful childhood experience and imagine it as a pebble dropped in a big pond of emotion. See the rings of waves spreading out from the point of contact of the stone. Unlike an actual pond, however, which quickly returns to stillness, we continue to feel these emotional ripples echoing through us until we are able to see them and calm them with our silent observation.

We should try to be patient with ourselves and all others and have compassion for the pain suffered so long ago that is creating these waves of emotion that are affecting us today. We can learn to let these ripples within us subside again and again, until they are lost in the firm banks of our own self-acceptance. Then, the pond that we are will be still.

*

We have to find the courage to be present with ourselves when we are feeling lost and alone - when our inner pond is astir - and to also remember that we have the universe guiding us in every moment. We can learn to hold our own hand through the days of darkness and know that although we cannot always see the sun, it is shining. Every treasure has a path leading to it and if we continue walking this path back into ourselves, we will find greater inner peace, happiness and connection with ourselves and others.

*

We all have a choice to live alone or in community with the world. To choose the latter we have to practice forgiving others for their actions and do what we can to help them and ourselves. In addition to offering our peaceful thoughts, we can look for ways to be in creative action so that we can improve someone else's experience in this moment, and as a result, our own. Doing this provides us with an opportunity to realize how much selfishness and aggression destroy our world and how much power we have to stop it. By simply sharing our generous thoughts and empowered, caring actions with others and ourselves, the world will be reborn.

5

The Power of Acceptance

Taking care of an animal such as a puppy can teach us to become more accepting, caring, and patient. Or it can leave us feeling even more unhappy, overburdened, and stressed. It is important to remember that a puppy is just like a human. It needs time to grow, to make mistakes, to learn, and be nurtured. We can't rush the rate at which a puppy learns and grows any more than we can make rain fall from a sunny sky. In order to fully understand this, however, we also have to be willing to grow and learn, especially if we have led very focused and self-centered lives. We need to grow to accept all of the puppy's experiences, just as we must learn to accept our own.

And just as a puppy is sometimes going to make a mess when we don't want them to, we are also occasionally going to make mistakes when we don't want to. We cannot always act in ways that we would like. If we can remember this, we will take a lot of weight off of our shoulders and be able to more readily accept the puppy and ourselves as we are in every moment - sometimes happy, sometimes whining, sometimes playful, sometimes sad.

*

When we are able to accept all of our different experiences, like we might those of a puppy, we can begin learning from them and grow in wisdom and insight. As we do this, we will begin to feel more empowered and can start taking real responsibility for our lives. When we begin letting ourselves be exactly as we are in any moment, we can start embracing all of our emotions and begin to see our inner world as a wonderful classroom to explore. By looking at our lives in this way, the need to satisfy ourselves with things outside of us will decrease and we will be more accepting of life exactly as it is – and we will be able to enjoy that puppy and our own lives even more.

6

We Are Enough

We are constantly comparing ourselves to other people and looking for something to do or something to consume that will cover up our uncomfortable emotions and make us feel like we have enough, like we are enough.

*

We always want more and can never seem to remember that we are perfect exactly as we are. We tend to be blinded by our desire for achievements and acquisitions, and forget that even without these things, we are enough.

We can perhaps see this more clearly if we consider a baby. We wouldn't judge a baby's worth based on her possessions or surroundings. Even if a child had been born into poverty, with parents who were neglectful, she would be of no less worth than the child of caring, wealthy parents. Regardless of their situations, you would hopefully agree that they were both of the same value - equally able to give and receive love.

But all too often we do judge people, even children, based on their appearances or their economic situations. It is almost as if we don't want their hard luck to rub off on us; as if we would rather push them away and stay in our self-concocted bubble of superiority and imagined perfection.

*

We tend to overlook the value that we all have simply because we are alive. We think that we always have to have more and that we have to be more; that we are never good enough or pretty enough or smart enough. We forget that there is nothing ugly or inferior that is born of nature. Only something that falls upon man's eyes gets classified as pretty or prestigious. Only humans are trapped in a world of dualism. A world of right and wrong. Happy and sad. Good and bad.

Do we think that a goldfish or a frog or a leaf on a tree can do anything bad? All that they can do is be. And all that they can be is what they are. Nothing more and nothing less. And they never feel awkward or out of place. Unless we cage them up and stare at them. Unless we take them out of being and try to put them into doing. Nice show dog. Nice trained bear. Nice tiger jumping through a hoop so that we can get money and fame and impress people and feel like the strongest animal and forget that we are equal to all living things.

Oh, yes, how superior we are - with all of the high-tech, entertaining products that we create and consume and discard. But can any of our inventions rival the simple complexities of a single delicate flower, moving in the wind, opening and closing as it knows it should?

Are we able to comprehend the magnitude and the wonder and the inconceivable richness of the world around us? Can we stand in amazement at a single blade of grass that knows somehow when spring is here and when it is time once again to sprout anew and grow again, reaching for the sun and the clouds that give it life, so that it may in turn give life?

*

And it is within all of this mystery that we find ourselves, thinking that we are better than the plants and the animals because we are smarter than them and can kill them and eat them, and unless we are unlucky, they can't do the same to us. And we think, perhaps, that they are simpler than us and that they have to obey our commands. Because we said so and we want to have things our way.

*

We want to always feel strong. And yet, still we feel weak. And still we feel afraid.

And still God sees us like everything else. All beautiful and all precious. All unique and all the same.

And still we see ourselves as competitors and countries.

As consumers and carpenters. As builders of our destiny and an evermore perfect life.

7

A Life of Abundance

When we are constantly looking outside of ourselves for things to make us feel happy, we can easily forget that we are already enough and become overly dependent on material possessions that we often don't really need. We can have trouble seeing that we are surrounded by other gifts of all sorts and become selfish and jealous of other people. We can also overlook the fact that life is not a zero sum game and that there is enough happiness for all. Until we stop taking from the world and comparing ourselves to others so much, however, we will never understand this or have what is truly important.

*

Many of us subconsciously believe that it is only after we become happy that those around us can feel the same. We may publicly support other people, but secretly envy them when they do succeed. Most of us would love to have more money or quality relationships, for example, but when we don't and see our close friends or relatives growing in these areas, we can sometimes start to feel jealous, scared, or lonely.

*

The unconscious desire that we often have to keep our environment the same, and this includes our friends and relatives, is often threatened by positive changes that they experience. In deep and subtle ways we can feel afraid of being left behind in an uncomfortable place that has been made more tolerable by the presence of someone else who was faltering alongside us. Our desire for this companionship, this solidarity in smallness, can be threatened when these people's lives improve.

For example, how would you feel if a long-time friend who shared your lonely fears of being single forever suddenly met a woman or man who fulfilled all of their dreams (and perhaps yours as well)?

Would you be filled with gratitude that someone so dear to you was experiencing and reflecting the possibility of greater happiness? Or would you feel uncomfortably alone, with a sense of urgency to also find a mate and not be "left out"?

Perhaps you would long for the days before things had changed. For the days when you and your friend were paddling the same boat of sadness and loneliness. And now, suddenly, you are alone in this boat. Can you accept that you are there instead of desperately searching the shore for a warm body upon which to land? Can you continue gently paddling and enjoy the ride and scenery and realize that it maybe isn't actually all that bad being alone? That your salvation doesn't necessarily lie in the arms of another.

Perhaps you can let your friend have their happiness and realize that it can in no way diminish your own. You see, happiness is something that there is an unlimited supply of.

*

It is important to remember that a happy, fulfilled world will always be a better place to live in. When people feel happier, they are naturally more generous, open, and easy-going, so we should always wish the best for our friends, family, and acquaintances. By doing this, we will brighten our world and more clearly understand the potential for happiness that our own lives hold. When we allow others to have their happiness, we can more easily feel as if we are enough and begin to see that their joy cannot limit our own.

There is no pleasure in hanging onto smallness. Let yourself fly and encourage those around you to find their wings.

8

The Wisdom of Change

We must learn to let it be okay to make mistakes; to grow and stumble and change. We must learn to embrace change as something that is helpful and good. Change is, of course, the only constant, and the sooner we are willing to accept not only its inevitability, but the power it holds, we can begin to free ourselves from much unnecessary pain.

As our outer situation changes, we must adjust our inner perspective. The more that we can do this - adapt to change - the more we can begin to see that it is okay to always be different and always be changing.

*

And this process of embracing change is inherently one of making mistakes. As we learn to adapt to each new situation, we often stumble and falter before we become comfortable in our new reality. Yet, it is vital to make mistakes, as each one is like a seed that gets planted within us. As we navigate the garden of life, we can eventually begin avoiding those plants which can cause us suffering and pain, for we are able to recognize them as plants which we already have growing within our field of wisdom. If we fail to acknowledge the inevitability of our mistakes, however, we are destined to live a life of regret, with any growing opportunities and wisdom building moments seen as simply more struggles and hopeless roadblocks on the path to happiness. As our wisdom grows, however, through the acceptance of our mistakes, we can begin to see them instead as helpful companions on our life's journey.

And just as a skier can learn to feel comfortable on very challenging slopes, we can learn to glide through life, listening to our inner sense of direction. As we honor our inner wisdom and further nurture it by not beating ourselves up over mistakes we might have made, but by accepting these experiences for the wisdom they hold, we can begin to work with life on its own terms.

As we continue learning from our mistakes, our well of wisdom deepens and our sense of direction and the ability to trust our instincts improves. We begin to feel not so helpless and alone, and find it easier to embrace change, for we understand that through change we often make mistakes, learn, and grow ever so slowly wiser.

*

As we become more aware of our ever-changing inner world, we can begin accepting both our vulnerabilities and our strengths, and see life as an opportunity to acquire both humility and wisdom. We can begin recognizing the perfection of each moment, and start accepting ourselves exactly as we are, realizing that we are already enough. The need to satisfy ourselves with outer stimulus will decrease and we will become happier and more comfortable within our own bodies, continuously moving ever closer to an honest expression of our true self. We will begin to take greater responsibility for our lives, and move in directions that offer us more happiness and fulfillment.

*

As we begin opening to change and acknowledging our inner truths, we can begin to re-define ourselves according to an inner sense of which direction our lives should head. We can do this by listening closely to our hearts and moving in directions that feel right. We can begin following the impulses from within - the longings of our heart and soul. You see, we all have unique gifts that we can share with the world, but to discover these talents, we must first know who we truly are. As we become more comfortable with all of our emotions, we can begin sensing which paths feel right to us and courageously begin following them.

*

We must remember, however, that our mind is a very impatient thing and we must always be on guard against making unhealthy decisions that arise from being in an uncomfortable mental or emotional state. Change for change's sake is often the result of discomfort within us. Change to mask discomfort will usually not benefit us. It will often only add further instability and fear into our lives. We should recognize when change is necessary and when instead it might make more sense to stay with an experience until we have investigated it fully. For example, if we find ourselves wanting to run from a situation before we have expressed our true feelings and tried to change it, we might be using change to mask our own discomfort. By doing this, we may simply be delaying a lesson that life is trying to provide us.

Often it is prudent to try to change a situation before we abandon it. At the very least, this will make any decision to leave that we do make feel more right inside of us because we will know that we haven't run from life. To encounter situations that we don't like or can't accept and to try and change them gives us a sense of confidence and self-worth that can only be realized by meeting life on its own terms.

*

As we learn to welcome change into our lives, we can begin to feel less resistant to challenging situations that we encounter and instead view them as opportunities to take action in ways that empower us. When we realize that change is constant, we can embrace it and become a part of it, and begin moving in directions that are more fulfilling and authentic.

9

Choosing Awareness

Do you find life difficult at times? Do you often wish things were different than they are? Do you ever become frustrated in traffic and find it hard not to honk your horn out of anger? Do you occasionally (or frequently) feel boredom, loneliness, or sadness?

If you happened to answer yes to one or more of these questions, you are well on your way to succeeding in this thing called life. You are already out of the gate and on the path to inner peace and fulfillment. Congratulations!

And for those of us who are still having trouble answering yes, have you ever, even for a moment, felt tired, satisfied, or excited?

Okay then, I think we have got everyone up to speed.

*

Now, if you are wondering what the point of all those questions was, please let me explain...

That little quiz you just passed was an acknowledgment that you are alive and that your days are filled with a constant array of sensations and feelings.

In accepting this fact, we can start to move beyond blindly reacting to our inner world and begin learning from it. And lucky for us, we have been given a big gift to help us do this. This gift is called life; the teacher that everyone loves and sometimes hates, the teacher we are all blessed with for our whole time on this earth.

*

Whether we are aware of it or not, every moment in our lives is perfectly designed for our growth. There are no mistakes in our curriculum. There are no misprints or imperfections. Life is constantly supporting us and providing us with experiences that are expressly created for our exact needs at all times. And yet, we resist the ones that cause us discomfort and crave those that give us pleasure. We fuss and fidget like a three year old way in over his head with his A,B,C's. We get to the letter B - or perhaps the letter from the bank - and start squirming like our pants are on fire. We then invariably start searching through the fridge or the channels on the TV, looking for something to satisfy us, to fill us up, to take us away from our uncomfortable feelings of sadness, loneliness, and fear. By doing this, however, we are actually running from ourselves and the chance to know our true nature. And the place that we are running from is the place that we are going to learn to run back to. That is, we are going to start running back to ourselves, instead of toward external sources of illusory comfort.

*

To help you better understand what this means, please close your eyes and for a count of five in-breaths, focus all of your attention on your breath as it moves in and out of your nose.

Now obviously this is quite simple, but it can also be very difficult at the same time. Perhaps not for five breaths, but if we do this same exercise for a bit longer, things can become somewhat trickier. Why don't you try it again and see if you can keep all of your attention totally on your breath for five minutes... Just keep watching your breath going in and out, in and out, and in and ... "Wait, what was that sound? Oh, it's just the fridge." And back and forth, in and out, and in and ... "Boy my leg is itching, it seems like it's tingly... I wonder if it's falling asleep? Maybe I should move it because I hate that burning sensation that I always feel when... oops, I forgot about my breath"... in and out... in and out...

And how did it go? Perhaps you saw how much there is going on inside of you and around you. And maybe you discovered how easy it is to become sidetracked by those things - how the mind can quickly become distracted, constantly jumping around like a curious little monkey. Maybe you also realized how you were able to bring your awareness back to your breath; that it can be like an anchor, a place to bring your attention back to when it strays. And maybe you noticed that some thoughts brought up uncomfortable sensations within you or maybe very pleasurable ones. In fact, there are many things that you might have seen. However, if you hadn't taken the time to close your eyes and look inside, it all would have gone on without you. That is, you would have had the same thoughts and the same sensations and the same fears, but you would have blindly followed them without evening knowing it. For just as our mind is automatically drawn toward whatever catches its attention, so, too, are we unwittingly pulled wherever our mind goes. And unless we make a choice to notice how this is happening, we will never even realize that it is.

*

But we do have a choice in every moment - one that can lead us back into ourselves so that we can find our way out of our old habits and negative patterns. One that can show us who we truly are, beyond the years of unconscious habits and beliefs that we have stored away deep within us. This choice is the choice of awareness, or in particular, self-awareness - of our thoughts, our feelings, and our sensations.

*

As we start to become aware of our constantly changing inner world of thoughts and emotions, we can then begin consciously observing them and growing in presence. And as we do this, we can slowly start to learn from our inner experience and begin responding to it with wisdom and compassion, instead of blindly reacting to it.

It is with this choice that we can begin unlocking our self-limiting patterns and our lost potential for true health, happiness, and fulfillment.

And this choice is ours in every moment.

It is the key to our freedom and the path to our heart's desire.

*

As we begin acknowledging the power that we hold in our own hands and learn to unleash it by focusing our awareness on our inner workings, we can begin learning from every situation. We can begin to see that true happiness is found by looking within us, and learn to not judge our judgments or hate our hate. We can discover that the path to true strength, understanding, and fulfillment is the one that is in front of us in every moment. And we can realize that this moment is another opportunity to accept and acknowledge our right, our choice, and our need to investigate, understand, and embrace whatever it is that we might find within us. And as we begin doing this, life will become a class where the subject is constantly changing, and if we are paying attention, no lesson is boring. Not even the one on boredom.

10

Moving Out of Reaction

Our emotions are constantly on parade within us, but we often become too overwhelmed by the fireworks and fanfare of our first reaction to something to simply observe them. For example, when another driver insults us by gesturing or honking, we may find ourselves instantly wanting to react out of anger or fear. In this type of situation, we are often quick to jump to defensiveness or accusing others of being at fault. We must remember, however, that we have a choice in every moment to either engage and add fuel to our emotions or to learn from them and let them go.

It takes a wise individual to recognize the path that their reaction wants to take them down. It takes great courage and resolve to say to oneself, "I know where this frustration and anger is going to lead, and as much as my wounded ego wants to go there, I won't let it."

*

As we become more aware of ourselves, we will begin to see how we often come into situations with pre-programmed reactions, acting almost as if we were on auto-pilot. We will also start to notice how easy it can be to lose ourselves in these reactions. And we will begin to see how limited many of them truly are.

We will also start to understand the reasoning, perhaps, behind many of our reactions that have long gone unrecognized and unchecked. And we will also begin to see how many of them are selfish and unjustified in nature, and how in many situations we may be acting without any sincere compassion or awareness of other people or their needs.

*

Certain individuals bring out uncomfortable feelings within us, and out of fear and impatience with our inner experience, we often react in ways that are designed to push these people away. We should realize, however, that not only are we avoiding life and relationships of substance with others by avoiding our unpleasant feelings, we are also avoiding ourselves.

When we react like this, it is almost as if we are trying to create some kind of protective bubble around us where no uncomfortable emotions will be able to find us. By doing this, however, we can become controlling or avoidant, and waste tremendous reserves of energy and creative potential in the process. The reasons for doing this often make perfect sense, however, as we frequently engage in this type of behavior to protect us from having to feel certain emotions that we had trouble assimilating at some earlier time in our lives. We tend to keep alive within us the emotional charge of any experience that we were unable to handle when it first occurred. Because we were not able to naturally integrate and release these feelings, we unconsciously hold on to them and do everything in our power to avoid having to face them again. But, of course, we will face them again. The universe wants us to accept all of our emotions and is constantly providing us with experiences to help us do this. We often seem to look for these situations unconsciously and yet are so surprised when we find ourselves in the same old familiar patterns.

*

In order to begin liberating ourselves from these patterns, we must first identify them. We must spend time searching our past and looking for ways in which life has provided us with similar lessons to learn. We can then heed their wisdom and direction, and take conscious action in order to avoid repeating them.

*

Life is compassionate and yet sometimes the lessons we receive seem to be particularly harsh and painful. Perhaps we might consider that life gives us exactly what we need and that sometimes we need a big push to open us up to a part of ourselves that we have long refused to acknowledge. By seeing things in this way, we can begin appreciating the deeper meaning behind every situation we encounter and start being more accepting and nurturing of ourselves, and eventually move beyond the inner patterns that are keeping us from realizing our true potential.

*

We tend to think of pain as something to be avoided at all costs. The truth is that no one is asking us to unnecessarily suffer or be helpless, but to realize that we might enjoy our lives more and be able to relate to ourselves and others in more fulfilling ways if we stopped our futile search for comfort and began stating our feelings instead of acting out our frustrations. If we began accepting life as our teacher and started paying attention to its lessons instead of ignoring them or complaining about them.

Behind every situation that we encounter is an opportunity to learn, grow, and further explore who we are, and to see how we may be acting in ways that are keeping us from living up to our potential.

We have the choice in every moment to learn from life and begin watching it unfold and help us, no matter how much we would prefer to run from the discomfort it sometimes offers.

*

As we begin to see how situations and people, by being exactly as they already are, can offer us a deeper awareness into our own lives, we can stop running from them and pushing them away.

As we begin to understand our own seemingly involuntary reactions to life's situations, we can grow in compassion for ourselves and for others who, like us, are often acting in ways that are designed to keep their unwanted emotions away.

*

We often criticize other people when we get caught up with one of their dysfunctional coping mechanisms. We might, instead of reacting to them with contempt or condescension, open ourselves up to a greater awareness of the hidden pain and fear that is propelling so many of their behaviors. By doing this, we can begin to understand how at times we are all seemingly ruled by some unseen hand within and learn to respond to their behaviors, and our own, with greater empathy and compassion.

*

As we begin acknowledging our own fears and desires, we can more easily recognize them in others. This will enable us to look beyond their actions and recognize the pain that may be causing them. By doing this, we will empower ourselves, for when we are able to see the unconscious motivators behind another's actions, we can begin to understand the impersonal nature of their ways. The slights and barbs that we encounter can perhaps be seen as calls for help or love; attempts to show us how uncomfortable these people truly are.

*

By looking at our lives in this way, we can, instead of feeling sorry for ourselves and becoming so easily upset at others, begin learning and growing from our interactions with them. We can start understanding the potential that we hold within us for liberation of the highest form. And we can start working with the conditioned reflex of unconsciously reacting with frustration and helplessness, and instead, begin seeing challenging people and situations as opportunities to grow and become more balanced and whole.

*

When we are able to notice how we want to react to life and instead choose to investigate and accept our feelings, we can start to respond to it from a place of inner wisdom and strength. We can then more easily begin allowing others to be who they are and learn to co-exist with them in an assertive manner. This will empower us and help us see more clearly our own roles and responsibilities in every situation.

*

As we learn to look within rather than simply reacting unconsciously to external situations, we initiate a chain of events that leads to a greater awareness of who we are and of how we might be more in control of ourselves in any situation. As we do this, we can start listening to and trusting our inner compass and acting in ways that feel truthful to us. We can slowly emerge from our life-long patterns and begin embracing those very elements within us that we have, for so long, avoided acknowledging. We can start to see life as a friend and teacher instead of an enemy and roadblock. We can begin working with it, instead of resisting it, and let it shape us in ways we could never have imagined.

*

As we begin observing ourselves in this way, we may start to realize how much unnecessary pain we have been causing ourselves and others by not acting authentically. We might also find sadness arising at wasted years or lost relationships. We should always remember to be gentle with ourselves and to realize that it is never too late for liberating change to occur.

This is an opportunity for those of us who have tasted life in all of its pain and pleasure to set aside the false security and optimism that our youthful sense of infallibility may have provided, and to begin learning from life and accepting how it truly is, rather than how we would prefer it to be. Experience and age can definitely be a virtue rather than an impediment on this inner path.

This process is one of acceptance and courageous change regardless of our age. It is about healing ourselves and our relationship with life, and learning to run to ourselves, instead of toward outer temporary sources of pleasure. It is about accepting life on its own terms, no matter what they may be, and letting all of our experiences be assets rather than liabilities.

*

As we begin letting our lives be exactly as they are, regardless of how much adversity and pain they may contain, we can start the long and beautiful journey out of our suffering.

We can let ourselves be touched by life, as it has been always trying to do, instead of avoiding the reality of our situation.

*

As we begin acknowledging all of our feelings rather than unconsciously reacting to them, we unleash a determined objectivity that enables us to learn and grow and move on to our next experience.

Instead of avoiding our pain and weakness, we can begin accepting it and learning from it. And slowly, by listening to our inner voice of truth, start changing in ways that enrich and enliven us.

*

Every time we focus only on those things that someone else is doing that are upsetting us and fail to investigate our own reaction to them, we ultimately remain helpless and ineffective, and lose an opportunity to learn more about ourselves.

"But that person is really acting hurtful or annoying," we might say.

Well, life would reply, "Yes, they are indeed."

And yet, how we want to change them! How we want to blame them for making us feel small, helpless, and uncomfortable.

*

The truth may very well be that the words and actions of another person do create some unpleasantness within us. But it is what we do with this discomfort that matters. Do we react blindly and act controlling or helpless, pushing that person or our true feelings away out of fear and imagined weakness? Or do we realize that we might benefit from acknowledging and accepting the uncomfortable emotions that their actions are stirring up within us? Do we allow these "undesirable" feelings to be present?

*

Perhaps we can let ourselves be touched by our emotions. Maybe we can let it be okay to feel the anger, jealousy, or fear right where it is (because where else could it possibly be?) and begin the beautiful process of watching it, listening to it, and learning from it.

Maybe we can begin asking ourselves, "What are these emotions trying to teach me and why are they such a strong charge within me? Why do they make me so uncomfortable? And in what ways might I be trying to avoid feeling them?"

Over time we can begin to simply watch our emotions arise and learn to be at peace with them, to smile at them even. "Ah, yes," we might say, "there is my old friend impatience, what does he have to show me about myself today?"

*

As we begin embracing the reality of our lives instead of simply reacting to them, we can turn our focus from one of being a victim to being a co-creator. We can begin letting all of our emotions in, so that they can lead us to a greater acceptance and love of ourselves and others.

We can begin allowing life to be as it is without pushing it away or running from it. And we can start seeing the truth within us and begin pulling the weeds of reactivity from our internal garden and begin replacing them with beautiful seeds of responding and right action.

We can start accepting responsibility for how we act and how we feel and begin behaving in ways that are true to ourselves and others.

And we can start expressing how we actually feel in ways that are strong, yet gentle, firm in conviction, and balanced in truth.

*

Avoiding our discomfort is actually keeping us from truly knowing and accepting the depth of peace and joy that is our birthright. Just as a weightlifter must endure the pain and struggle of exercise before being rewarded with a healthy, strong body, we, too, must exercise our ability to let the reality of life in - with all of its pain and pleasure - before we can be rewarded with peace and happiness.

Until we stop sitting on the fence and begin exploring the fields of both our "good" and "bad" emotions and experiences, we will remain locked in a small shell of our true potential.

*

Life is waiting for you to dance with her. Please come away from the security of the walls that you have created to keep her out and let her sweep you off of your feet.

11

Living Our Truths

Many of us make our way through the day with a pretend smile on our face, projecting an image of politeness. Or perhaps we put on a different face in public - one of anger and tightness. Perhaps we act in ways that are designed to make sure we never get hurt, such as hiding behind an expression of unfriendliness. No matter how we choose to act in public, however, when we do so, we are being untrue to ourselves and our real feelings.

As we begin following our instincts and learn to express our feelings, no matter how uncomfortable that may be, we can put down our public facade. We can begin truly engaging in life and move beyond a false sense of politeness or anger.

*

When the only acting we do is on our feelings, we can stop living in masked anger and fear, and start responding to each new situation from a place of integrity. We can let go of the need to please others or push them away, and begin feeling more comfortable within ourselves. As we start behaving in ways that feel truthful to us, we will begin to trust that we will be able to deal with life as it is presented to us. We will also learn to better accept people as they are and allow our inner truths to guide us in every moment.

*

As we continue looking within and exploring our reactions to others' behaviors, we may discover that we are being overly sensitive to some issue because of a past experience of our own and that those people who are offending us are perhaps hurting in some way themselves. By acknowledging our emotions and asserting how we feel, we will no longer have to act in ways that are untrue for us. We will begin to feel less alone and vulnerable to the emotional whims of others and may find that we no longer have to pretend to be kind to others, for that will naturally become the most comfortable way to live.

As we move closer to our true selves by embracing our emotions and learning to express them, we may one day be able to wander through a room full of unfriendly people and not take any of it personally. We will better understand and have compassion for their suffering and see them as people who are unhappy and in pain. We may also find that we won't even have to complain about their behavior once we realize that they are not able to darken our day unless we let them. In this way, as we become stronger within ourselves, we can, in effect, walk through an otherwise lonely rain storm and never get wet.

*

Yet, perhaps there are still times when we do feel hurt by the words or actions of another. What are our choices in those moments? Please stop and take some time to think about this. Maybe set down your book and think of several ways that you would respond if, say, a librarian was pre-occupied and somewhat rude to you.

Our first reaction might be to feel insulted and angry, and that is perfectly normal. As we have spent so much of our lives looking for love, approval, and nurturance from the world around us, it is only natural to be somewhat taken aback when we don't receive these things.

Now, instead of reacting blindly to these emotions, take a moment and observe them. Notice what is going on inside for you. Become aware of your inner world and the emotions and sensations that you are experiencing. In this case, you might quietly and patiently say to yourself, "Hmm, I see anger and shame rising up, and in this moment they are quite strong, especially shame." By responding in this way, we can learn to automatically step back into ourselves, notice what we are feeling, and then plan our next move.

If we aren't being mindful, however, we might huff off silently and carry the insult around with us, not even acknowledging how we truly feel. Instead, we might let our emotions out around those we feel more comfortable with, such as our spouses, children, or pets. By realizing this, we can begin to see how much of the violence and abuse in our world could be stopped if people began accepting how they truly felt and learned to deal with their emotions instead of throwing them on others.

*

And how exactly are we supposed to "deal" with our emotions. Sounds like quite a soft and psychoanalytical way to live, doesn't it? Quite "touchy-feely" and new age... Well, it isn't.

To understand and use our inner compass, which is shown to us constantly through our sensations and feelings, makes us a warrior of the highest order. Men, women, and children who are taking responsibility for their words, actions, and feelings are doing the most difficult thing that any human being can do.

Facing our inner world is trial by fire; it is embracing life and being unable to move from the task at hand. Looking always deeper with eyes and heart that grow ever stronger, clearer, and compassionate is not a path for the faint of heart.

This is the most difficult thing that anyone can do and is in no way dependent on outer strength or macho bravado. In fact, men may have a harder time, at least initially, moving onto this path because our society falsely honors blind bravery, coldness, and an unwillingness to bend in its sons, and increasingly, in its daughters. For every cold-eyed soldier who is taught to abandon his feelings, we have another person who has closed himself off to his true potential and, ironically, to the most advanced weapon he could ever possess. This is a weapon of unlimited strength, yet it cannot be used to slay an enemy or conquer a neighboring land. This weapon - our own self-awareness - can be used to turn darkness into light and wrong into right. And the more we unleash it, the more we begin to see how any act of destruction is detrimental to all. This weapon would convince all soldiers to drop their arms and use their energy to mend and heal their differences instead of reinforcing them.

So for men who have long been taught to act in ways that are hard and silent, please have patience. Please understand that by choosing this weapon of truth and compassion, you are doing the most important thing possible for yourself, your brothers, your sisters, and your world.

*

We must learn to respect our feelings and sensitivities, and realize that there is nothing wise or strong about stumbling around in the dark just because we're too manly (or scared) to turn on the light.

And our ability to bring our awareness to the reality of all of our emotions, to acknowledge and embrace them, is our light switch. And it takes more courage than most are aware they possess to reach for this switch time and again, moment after moment.

*

When we are seemingly caught in a difficult inner situation, the first step we have to take is to admit that it is a difficult inner situation. We must be willing to accept that at times we are uncomfortable being filled with painful emotions. We need to acknowledge the difficulty we have being present with ourselves when our inner world is upset. This is the first step in being true to ourselves, in being a champion of our spirit.

*

When we experience an uncomfortable emotion, such as anger or shame, we must first accept that we are feeling it. This can be one of the most difficult steps, for our ego and pride do not enjoy being stirred up in this way. We may falsely believe that we are above life, that we shouldn't have to encounter any discomfort as the result of another's behavior. And how we squirm when we do! We want to lash out, fight back, or retreat ashamedly and lick our wounds. And we may want to hold onto the anger or fear. This situation threatens to destroy our inner peace, our whole day, or even longer. Our inner child and our fragile ego have been hurt, and damn it, they are going to let us know it. And, unconsciously, we let them take over. Falling prey to their temper tantrum, we engage in one of our own - huffing and puffing in anger or silently feeling resentful and sorry for ourselves.

And yet, herein lies a great insight. We don't have to act like small children, crying over simple slights. We can, instead, hold our inner pain as a parent might hold a wounded child. Although we can't take the child's pain away, we can be present for them. We can offer them compassion and acceptance and allow them to express themselves and their feelings in our safe and loving arms. And to be this parent, we simply have to observe ourselves, to be with ourselves.

*

The next time we get angry, perhaps we can try watching it for a moment before letting it overwhelm us. If we are able to sit with the anger - and one way of doing this is to notice which particular sensations we are feeling - we can begin to discover the calm,

49

eternally patient, and loving parent that exists inside all of us. We can begin to see how we might distance ourselves from the need to blindly react to our inner pain and discomfort. We can learn to stay with ourselves in a nurturing, loving, and very brave way, instead of squirming and lashing out in retaliation at having our false sense of inner peace disturbed. We can begin to understand how true peace and strength are found by observing our inner workings and start to develop a sense of presence in any situation. We can begin responding to life and to ourselves with maturity, compassion, and self-respect.

*

And so, we enter step two of our library experience. Taking into consideration everything we have just read, we can begin to see that a world of opportunities and options are open to us in every moment.

We can begin to find a sense of empowerment in our ability to act in ways which are truthful to us. We can start to trust ourselves and let go of our old patterns of reacting and behaving in ways that have, for a long time, caused us and those around us harm.

We can begin to understand the opportunity that life is handing us in every moment to grow and change, and we can start learning from our every encounter.

We can let our emotions be exactly as they are and mindfully choose how we might respond to them. We can discover a sense of empowerment and liberation that is born of the awareness that we are no longer slaves to life or our emotions. We can begin to act in ways that feel right and that help us and those we encounter.

*

Whenever we notice uncomfortable feelings rising up within us, we can choose which step to take next. Often the best choice is to take some time to investigate the situation and determine why it has stirred up our emotions. We should always do our best to look behind the scenes to see if we can figure out what is actually going on for us.

In the case of the librarian, we might choose to let his or her behavior go, knowing that if this person were happier in their own life, they would probably treat others better. Or maybe we would calmly and firmly state our feelings and needs in order to assert our desire to be treated with respect. Or perhaps we would smile, walk away, and come back with a small bouquet of flowers to brighten their day. Or maybe we would react in the same old way by lashing out or hiding our pain within us.

*

No matter our response or reaction to any situation, we should remember to be gentle with ourselves. We do not have to hurt ourselves needlessly. We do not have to live a life of tightness, smallness, and pain because of some uncomfortable experience, no matter how important it seems at the time.

Perhaps the thing that we are hanging on to and hurting ourselves over will be forgotten in five, ten, or twenty years. Or perhaps five, ten, or twenty minutes. Whatever the case, why not choose to let it go now and move on with our lives? Why not embrace the next situation afresh, wiser in the knowledge that life has given us? Why not look around for our next lesson? Why not touch our souls by being grateful for the patience and commitment that we have shown to ourselves? Why not continue to grow, instead of letting a past hurt or defeat keep us locked in the same old place? Perhaps we can allow the discomfort of an uncomfortable experience to be within us for a while, instead of attempting to silence the feelings life is trying to get us to accept.

*

As we embrace ourselves and acknowledge all of our emotions, we open our hearts to joy, sadness, and the entire experience that is our life. As we feel our fears and live our truths, we allow our past to lead us toward a better future. As we begin accepting whatever we are feeling in any moment, our pain will slowly heal and we will grow in happiness and inner peace.

As we continue doing this, we will realize that self-love is found in every step that we take toward greater acknowledgement and acceptance of our thoughts and our feelings. Our fears and our desires. Our loves and our losses.

12

Surrendering to Life

When our intentions and desires come into conflict with the natural flow of the universe, we will experience discomfort. As we become aware of this inner resistance, we can either ignore it and stay on our current path and keep acting in ways that are willful or we can begin acknowledging our emotions and surrendering to reality. By following the second path, we will be aligning ourselves with the depth of our experience in every moment and opening to greater connection with ourselves and life.

*

When times are difficult for us, we can choose to learn and grow from every situation. We can embrace life and let it shape us. We can look for opportunities in our moments of suffering and allow them to point us in directions that offer us greater peace and fulfillment. We can begin to see our painful experiences as calls from life; calls to wake up to our true path and our true potential.

*

If we are unwilling to acknowledge our emotions and question our intentions, however, we will never see life as a friend and teacher.

Our one option will be to continue struggling upstream alone while our connection to life and our true potential drift away from us. When we can begin to admit that things aren't always going to go our way, however, and start accepting the discomfort these moments might create within us, we can begin engaging in an unfolding unto our true selves and start working with life, rather than forging our path alone. This is a beautiful opportunity that awaits us at all times, whether we are willing to see it or not.

*

Whether we choose to accept help from a higher power or plan on battling it out ourselves is our choice. The ballroom of perfection is where you already are. Do you want to continue stumbling along to the tune that only you can hear or are you ready to listen carefully to the orchestra of life and learn to dance to the beautiful song it is playing?

13

Conscious Relationships

In order to heal our relationships, we have to stay present with our emotions when other people make us feel uncomfortable. If we can do this, we will begin to understand what it means to understand. Typically, however, we choose to become defensive when charges of right and wrong are being volleyed about. Instead of acknowledging our true feelings, we tend to put the focus on how the other person is wrong and protect ourselves by fighting back or silently turning inward. And, of course, it is very tempting to do this when someone offends us. But what does this really achieve? Often only heightened conflict, prolonged inner strife, and mutual unhappiness.

Rather than fanning the flames of tension and discord, however, we can learn to bridge the gap of separation that exists between us at the best of times and open our hearts to our own and another's pain.

If we can allow the unpredictability of life to touch us and not react in anger, disbelief, or arrogance in those moments when we feel slighted, we will grow in understanding and acceptance of ourselves and others.

If we can accept our pain and the ways in which we have been hurt by another's actions, we can stay open to the reality of our experience and ever so gently put down the shields which have kept our egos safe and our tempers alive.

If we are able to truly acknowledge our wounds, we can slowly open to the possibility of forgiveness; to finding the courage to wish happiness upon those who we think have wronged us.

*

Although it is very difficult, it is altogether possible to reach out from behind our bruised and defensive egos and try earnestly to understand our own and another's feelings. To do this, patience is needed, as is a desire to accept our own indignation.

Unless we can sit with our own anger, embarrassment, and fear upon hearing someone's accusations, we will never be able to build a bridge between us and will stay locked in our defensive isolation.

In simpler terms, we need to take it upon ourselves to let go of our need to always be right and to make others wrong. We must find the courage to be the first to lay down our arms and extend an understanding hand.

*

If we remain trapped in our emotions and fail to disassociate with them by mindfully observing them and changing the way we respond to them, we will remain angry and at the emotional mercy of others. By not honoring our own pain, we will only carry it around, perhaps to use in the future - to be able to say, "You hurt me once and I am still hurting from it and holding on to it."

If we are able to liberate ourselves from our unconscious reactions, however, we will lose the desire to judge others as we have long judged ourselves. We will begin to understand that their actions are about them and will let go of the need for them to behave in any particular way.

*

The cauldron of inner acceptance is full of more ingredients than we might like to acknowledge. We imagine that our uncomfortable feelings will hurt us, but it is in the avoidance of them that we do real harm. This unwillingness to acknowledge our emotions can result in a negative action being directed toward another or toward ourselves - both ways in which we avoid investigating those parts of us that we have labeled as undesirable.

*

We need to amend the reactive patterns in us that we learned as children. Without the responsibility of an adult, our inner children will run amok. Even though we may know that what we are doing is hurtful, we may still find ourselves wanting to grab from the outside to cover up the discomfort inside of us. And even when we can stop the drinking or the over-eating or whatever, we will still ultimately be stuck with ourselves. And unless we are prepared and willing to lovingly keep running to ourselves instead of the bar or

57

the fridge, we will continue to turn to some external avenue in an attempt to hide from our feelings.

*

Perhaps the most difficult thing that anyone can do is to sit with themselves. This is, of course, hard enough when we are alone and consciously determined to succeed. The real test is when life is our meditation room; when we try to bring an awareness and acceptance of our feelings to real life situations and our interactions with others.

We often exacerbate difficult situations in life by blindly reacting to them. If we can increase the time we spend observing our emotions in those moments when we are alone and "un-triggered", however, we will be much better prepared to respond in a mindful, compassionate, and assertive manner when we do encounter adversity in our lives.

*

We cannot hide from ourselves or from life. Every relationship that we have has been perfectly designed to push our buttons so that we can accept that we have them. We should do our best to allow those around us to be as they are and take courage and faith in knowing that they have been brought into our lives for our own growth.

We should also remember that we can only truly know and love another after we have learned to know and love ourselves.

It is important to keep our focus on unlocking the mystery that we are; on placing our attention on our own feelings and path in order to see it more clearly. We should do our best to lead our lives in ways that move closer to our own breath and our own heart; in ways that help us accept and nurture ourselves.

*

In the acceptance of our emotions and the relationships that bring them out in us, we can find wholeness, peace, and love. As we more fully begin to accept ourselves, we will move into a place of greater acceptance of all things and will begin to realize that compassion itself is born of acceptance - the acceptance of our fears, our desires and our destiny.

14

Conscious Communication

We have to stop hoping that others will act in ways that always leave us feeling good because, quite frankly, they won't. They can't. We often hurt each other out of fear and ignorance. This is a fact of life. We must not let it keep us down or alone. We shouldn't hide from this reality. Instead, we can learn how to communicate and set boundaries in ways that allow us to be a peaceful, strong presence of truth and acceptance in any situation. We can learn to be courageous within ourselves and clearly express who we are through our words and actions.

*

If we can begin stating our limits, needs, and feelings in ways that are believable, we will empower ourselves and feel more comfortable in all of our relationships. And in order to be believable, we have to be vulnerable and sincere – and the way to do that is by acknowledging and expressing our innermost truths. To hear these truths, we have to start listening to ourselves. With one ear tuned to our inner wisdom, we will know how to speak and act in ways that are authentic and appropriate. It simply takes practice and courage to do this.

*

When we are able to set healthy boundaries and explain what we are feeling and needing, it shows others that we know and respect ourselves and that we are to be respected. Expressing ourselves in this way also enables other people to drop their guard and to more easily trust us. In this way, they may be more able to understand our feelings and meet our needs as well. This is because we all instinctively respond better to hearing another's feelings and needs than to being yelled at or told we are wrong in some way.

*

It is important to own our emotions and our part in every situation. It is much more difficult to say what we actually feel and need than to engage in a battle of ego superiority. The simplicity of our true needs perhaps scares us. It may be shocking to realize that we don't require all of the painful fanfare of a full-blown argument or the short-term satisfaction and emotional release that our anger tossing allows.

*

To be able to see a difference brewing and not have to bring up past transgressions and instead simply say what we are feeling and needing helps us more effectively turn our differences into workable situations. This may seem challenging at first, but over time, we will learn how empowering it can be to communicate in this way.

*

To say no to the need to engage in a dysfunctional argument is very liberating. In order to do this sincerely and effectively, however, we must also acknowledge our own actions. We have to set down our defensiveness and say with sincerity that we are truly sorry if we have hurt the other person.

When we are able to stay with the present situation and not bring up past hurts or throw in new accusations and simply say, "I feel this, I need this, and perhaps you are quite right in saying that I have hurt you, and for that I am sorry", we can initiate a more honest and heartfelt dialogue and lead ourselves and others toward greater love, understanding, and empathy.

*

When two people commit to communicating in this way, their hearts and minds will open like a flower on a spring day! A relationship that is based on vulnerability, honesty, and trust is such a beautiful thing. When two people can let each other be who they truly are, no matter what they are feeling and experiencing - when they can simply hold space for the other and be present for them - they will have a remarkable opportunity to grow individually and together, and will learn the meaning of true acceptance, respect, and love.

*

In those difficult moments that have often led to tears, anger, and painful accusations in the past, we can begin to slowly find trust. As we begin expressing our needs and feelings in loving and understanding ways, we will gain confidence in our ability to respond appropriately to any situation. From a place of self-acceptance and strength, we will slowly move toward compassion and mutual respect.

*

As we are able to acknowledge and meet our own needs, we will also begin to realize that we need this less and less from others. We will also find that we are less affected by other people's behaviors and more able to see their positive attributes. We will have more understanding and empathy for their pain and the behaviors it creates in them. We will also be able to stop needing them to act in ways that for whatever reasons are impossible for them and will more readily be able to let them be who they actually are. By connecting with other people in this way, we will also be able to more clearly recognize the perfection of life and the lessons that are available to us in our every relationship and interaction.

*

We can complain all day about someone's behavior, but when we realize that setting our boundaries and sharing our feelings often only requires a few sincere words, we will spend less time looking for faults in others and more time accepting our own. We will begin growing in compassion for ourselves and everyone we encounter.

*

When we display our inner truths and self-respect through our words and actions, we automatically give those around us a framework in which to operate.

By expressing ourselves in ways that are honest and kind, we help state our needs much more effectively than a thousand screaming matches or misunderstood moments of uncomfortable silence ever could.

By acting in ways that show respect for ourselves, our feelings and our needs, we teach others how to do the same and will be able to experience greater love, connection, and peace in all areas of our lives.

15

Looking Into Our Story

As we begin to see ourselves more clearly, we can start to comprehend the power we possess to change our lives. With each step that we take toward liberating ourselves from blind judgments and unthinking acts, we free ourselves from the need to constantly react unconsciously to the world around us. We also begin to understand our unique nature and have an ever-clearer picture of ourselves.

As our old ways of craving and avoidance are brought to our attention, we can start to see how we can further liberate ourselves. And as we face our hidden fears and illusions and embrace the reality of our own lives, we can begin acting in ways that are more authentic and empowered. When we stop losing ourselves in external struggles and begin embracing our emotions and exploring our inner world, we will find ourselves on the path to true freedom.

*

It is important to realize, however, that investigating our inner world and facing our fears is not necessarily something that we will particularly like. Our mind and body may kick and scream as we expose them to fears that we have hidden from our whole lives.

Our mind might tell us that we are going crazy or are helpless or weak, all in an attempt to avoid growing and letting go of the lie that we are totally in control of our destiny.

But if we listen very closely, beyond our quivering body and defiant mind, we will hear our spirit saying, "Come on, you can do it," urging us on to greater and greater depths of freedom.

*

We all have the opportunity to be free. And to be free, we have to find the courage to face ourselves. We have to find the patience and determination to embrace whatever we discover with compassion and truth.

By exposing our inner world to the light of our awareness, freedom and fulfillment can be found.

*

We seem to constantly be looking outside of ourselves for answers, however. Be it a spiritual search or one solely for pleasure, we often tend to think that someone or something "out there" will solve our problems and make us feel better. We'd like to believe that just one more self-help book or one more sermon or one more relationship will make us feel better (or one more donut or beer...).

Of course, it is prudent to look for support from those who can help us to see our own truths; to help us unearth our own gold, so to speak. But remember, no one can do this inner work for us, no one can mend our soul as it were.

To realize our true potential, we must open up to all of the answers and possibilities that are already within us.

*

The path to true happiness can be found by discovering, accepting, and learning from our inner world. Seek people who can help you do this. Those individuals who can objectively help you to see the truth can be very important to you on your journey.

But know that you already have all of the answers inside of you and that life is designed to bring them into your view in every moment. This is why yoga and meditation can be so helpful; they are two important doorways to an inner world that we perhaps aren't even aware exists.

*

The truth is, we have to do the work of bravely looking into our own story and this can only be done by looking within ourselves and at our lives.

One way that we can do this is to look at the different people we know and ask, "How do they truly make me feel?" Perhaps ask yourself, "Does anyone leave me feeling insecure or awkward? Do I avoid spending time with them because they are mean to me, perhaps in subtle ways? Do my friends and family all treat me well? Do they accept who I am and encourage me to do whatever feels right - to be the person that I, or they, know I can be?"

And look for a moment at how you treat them. Do you belittle them for doing things differently than you? Do you get angry at them when things don't go your way? Do you find certain things about their behaviors challenging, but refuse to mention them? If so, why do you remain quiet? What does your silence represent? Are you afraid of conflict or do you consider it impolite to express how you truly feel? Are your relationships built on a foundation of vulnerability and truth or are they more shallow? Do you wonder who your friends really are behind their outer expressions? Do you put them or yourself in a "personality box" at all - he is this, she is that, and I am something else? And most importantly, can you accept and learn from any answers that arise from these questions?

*

As we begin looking into the reality of our own lives, we should do our best to stay focused on our own actions and the ways in which we treat those around us. Rather than attempting to control them, we should remain committed to change; to changing ourselves according to the truths that we discover within us.

*

As we become more aware of our inner world and our interactions with others, we can begin to see how all of our relationships can help us further liberate ourselves from our unconscious patterns and help us live in more peaceful and authentic ways.

We can also begin to realize how our lives can be like a petri dish in a giant laboratory and how we can become important scientists on a mission to find a cure for the most dangerous disease of all time: ignorance.

16

The Power of Giving

We often assume that money, success and material possessions will shield us from life's discomforts and the painful emotions that accompany them. We perhaps imagine that if we can control our environment, we can somehow hide from our unwanted feelings and remain in a constant state of pleasure.

And our world supports this. Advertisements constantly encourage us to buy this or do that, luring us toward ever-greater comfort. Yet, as we continue buying into them, we can quickly find ourselves trapped, thinking that if we keep consuming we will eventually become happy and whole.

But isn't it true that we do feel more excited and alive when we make a new purchase? Don't we actually feel as if we are more when we have more? If we look closely, however, we may see that on some level we are decorating our homes and filling up our closets so that we can always feel good. Now there is nothing wrong with a beautiful home or beautiful clothing or a new car. However, these things often become more than just useful and enjoyable objects - they become a way to cover up any discomfort that we feel within. Yet, we may find that we actually do feel better (or worse, if we are plagued with regret) after we eat a big meal or spend an afternoon buying clothes. But just as we will surely become hungry once again, that new dress or shirt we bought will inevitably become just another, like all the rest.

*

No matter what we have, it seems that we always want more. This constant state of desire not only deprives us of the ability to acknowledge that the possessions we already have are enough, but makes it very difficult to realize that we are also enough. When we base our self-worth on external accomplishments or the things that we have, we can quickly lose sight of the beauty that is found in every moment and the reality that we are already enough, exactly as we are.

*

Life is constantly providing us with situations that are designed to help us accept and learn from all of our emotions. Instead of embracing these opportunities, however, we often run from them, ignore them, or push them away. We tend to judge our emotions and spend much of our time chasing the good ones and avoiding the others. This is not unlike how we refer to rainy days as "terrible" and sunny days as "great". The truth, of course, is that sunshine is no better than rain; they are both important parts of our experience and we need both to survive. And just as we cannot harvest a rich crop in a dry desert (where, by the way, they often dance when the rains come - one man's pain being another's pleasure...), we cannot hope to find a rich and fulfilling life by only investing our time in activities that make us feel good.

*

71

As we begin letting go of our constant search for pleasure, however, and start embracing all of our emotions, we will find ourselves growing in awareness and inner peace and living more fully in the moment. As we start accepting our feelings instead of constantly resisting them and taking from the outside world to cover them up, we will discover a life of greater happiness and fulfillment. And we will also begin to understand that true happiness and fulfillment don't actually come from taking, but from giving.

By shifting our focus from taking to giving, we will start to heal our wounds and reclaim our inner peace and strength. We will begin integrating all of our emotions and become more balanced and whole. We will start living in greater harmony with ourselves and with life.

And while the opportunity to do this is available to each of us in every moment, because we may have spent so much of our lives taking, it might be hard to fully understand what it means to do this.

*

Perhaps the easiest and most important way to understand the power of giving is by looking at ways that we can give to ourselves in those moments when we are feeling uncomfortable emotions. Rather than taking away our power by running from them, we can instead begin giving to them – giving them our attention, acceptance, and love.

In order to begin giving to ourselves in this way, however, we have to decide that enough is enough and make the courageous decision to finally stop hurting ourselves and distracting ourselves no matter what might be happening in our lives, no matter what we might be feeling.

We also have to begin giving compassion to ourselves for those old ineffective and often painful ways that we used to express our emotions or find relief from them. And instead of continuing to engage in these activities, we have to simply choose to begin gently embracing whatever we might happen to be feeling and allow it to be exactly as it is - as it wants to be.

*

It is important to understand that we can't actually run or hide from our emotions. We have to realize that doing this, ultimately, will not help us. It will not work.

We have to, instead, begin accepting whatever we are experiencing and start being kind to ourselves. We have to start taking care of ourselves.

We have to begin gently holding all of our painful emotions with patience and purpose.

With love.

*

We also have to realize that if we keep taking and hurting ourselves with our overindulgences - if we keep numbing ourselves to our pain - we are only going to keep suffering.

Until we give our attention and acceptance to our discomfort – until we truly allow it to be - it will not shift.

Until we honor it and heal it by giving it our love, it will remain alive within us.

It will not go away.

*

As we begin to give acceptance, compassion, and love to ourselves, however, then our pain will begin to transform and we will start to heal. And then our scary emotions won't have to come around so often. Then they will begin to fade away.

Until we decide to give to ourselves in these ways, however, they will stick around because when we choose not to acknowledge our emotions – when we try to cover them up or run from them - we are really only just resisting them. And the more that we resist them, the more they will strengthen and build, which invariably will just make us want to run from them even more (can you spot the vicious cycle here?). And the more that we do that, the more they will just want to be heard and the louder they will become. The more desperately they will try to get us to hear their frightened calls and have us console them - to give them our attention and acceptance.

When we can be there for them, however, when we can give them our presence, patience, and love - like a parent would give to a child, they won't have to scream so loudly for our attention. They will feel seen and heard and begin to trust us, and we will begin to trust ourselves. And over time, they won't have to hang around so much, for when we let it be okay for them to stay, they won't need to. They'll be free to go. To move on.

And so will we. Finally unburdened by the weight of these different parts of our inner experience that we have been resisting for so long, we will be free to live in greater peace and more able to give to others and ourselves.

*

We have to realize, however, that, ultimately, no one else can do this for us. No one else can truly give us the love and attention we need.

Only we can do this. Only we can stop taking from the world to cover up our pain. Only we can stop hurting ourselves again and again. Only we can run to ourselves when we are upset. Only we can truly accept what we are feeling. Only we can remember to soften our body and our breath. Only we can turn the power of our awareness inward and gently hold ourselves like a parent would hold a scared and wounded child, compassionately soothing their fears and their pain.

Only we can truly take care of ourselves in these deep and beautiful ways.

Only we can truly love ourselves.

*

And this love that we can shine on ourselves is like no other. It is the most powerful and direct form of love that anyone can give us because, in its purest sense, it is free from the constraints that inhibit the love another person might be able to show us. For no matter who they are, no matter how emotionally healthy they are, and no matter how much they may love us, these other people are human and have their limitations. And most importantly, they are not us. They are not inside of us. They are separate from us. They will never know what we are feeling or understand our pain to the same degree that we can.

*

Other people cannot love us as deeply and purely as we can.

No one else can. Only we can.

Only we can shine the powerful light of our own love and awareness on our inner wounds. Only we can do this.

Only we can truly love ourselves.

*

So the next time you are experiencing unpleasant emotions, practice giving love to yourself.

76

Imagine that you are a child and do your best to gently hold yourself and all of your discomfort within your awareness.

Just do your best to feel it, to allow it to be.

*

Simply accept your pain. Just acknowledge that you are feeling whatever you are feeling. If you are scared, let it be okay to be scared. If you are angry, let it be okay to be angry.

Simply let it be okay to feel whatever energy you are experiencing and do your best to accept it.

And if you are having difficulty accepting the pain - if it is too strong or intense - then simply do you best to accept your inability to accept it. Just accept whatever you are experiencing with patience and compassion. Just give your awareness - your love - to whatever you are experiencing.

*

As we continue giving love and attention to ourselves in these ways, we will start to move out of our old patterns and begin integrating all of our emotions. We will start to feel more whole, empowered, and peaceful, and will be able to live more fully and authentically in every moment.

*

And this giving attitude is something that we can extend to other areas of our lives as well. In order to do this, we simply have to begin observing our actions and intentions as we make our way throughout each day. By engaging in this type of inquiry, we will discover how we might shift our perspectives and become more giving in heartfelt ways that leave us feeling more connected to ourselves, others, and life.

*

We can begin doing this by asking questions and investigating our attitudes about everything in our lives, including something as familiar as the food we eat. For example, do we choose our food based on its nutritional content and life giving properties or do we just take whatever happens to be quick and handy? And when we are eating, do we race through our meals or do we give ourselves the gift of savoring our experience? Do we give ourselves time to finish what we are chewing before taking another bite? And do we occasionally eat to numb away our fears or do we give ourselves healthy boundaries that honor all of our emotions? After all, we are not only what we eat, but how we eat. And why.

And we can extend these queries outward as well. For example, do we consider where the food we buy comes from and how our purchases give back to the economic system as a whole? Are we just taking from the corporate factory farms with all of their callous efficiency or are we giving our money to those farmers who are choosing to grow food in ethical ways where workers, animals, and crops are being given the gift of respect that they deserve? And are we considering how our food purchases affect the environment?

Are there ways that we might give back to it by making choices that support sustainability and the health of our planet?

And while these are just a few examples of how we might investigate but one area of our lives, there are countless ways that we can do this – just as there are countless ways that we can give.

*

We are constantly led to believe that something out there, something outside of us, will make us feel whole. Yet, it is in the act of giving that we can begin to more clearly understand our true selfless nature.

*

As we practice giving to ourselves and to life, we will begin to realize that our hearts and our minds are already full and we can begin caring instead of consuming, and giving, instead of grabbing.

*

We will also begin to realize that the only way that we actually can give is if we have enough. If we are enough.

And we are.

17

Navigating Our Inner World

As we stop taking from the external world and start saying no to those things outside of us that have tried to pull us away from ourselves for so long, we will begin to reclaim our inner power. As we learn to run to ourselves and start embracing and learning from all of our emotions, we will slowly begin finding our way out of our fear, negative patterns, and suffering. As we continue doing this, as we keep exploring and learning from our inner world, there are certain things that we may experience that are important to understand.

*

The first thing we should realize is that for every step forward we take toward shifting our unconscious, limiting patterns, we may at times experience a rebound of sorts, where the mind, wanting to revert to its old, familiar ways, lashes back in anger and helplessness at the prospect of impending change. One good way to avoid this growth rebound is to remember to be gentle with yourself when you are experiencing inner turbulence. It is important to realize that we don't have to add more pain to that which we are already feeling; we don't have to add any more resistance to our experience.

*

And if we are able to acknowledge that some days are going to be more challenging than others, then we can practice being grateful for those sunny days when we have clear vision and are glad to be alive. Then, if we once again begin to see new clouds within that surprise us with their persistence or their pain, we can try our best to accept them as they are. We can choose to see these potentially unpleasant experiences as valuable opportunities to learn how we may have been avoiding those very things which can help us find true freedom: our own confusion, pain, and suffering.

*

There may also be certain times on our inner journey when we are feeling extremely empowered by a particular insight and might almost believe that we have it all figured out, as if our inner work is nearly done. It is important to remember, however, that there are many steps on the path to inner peace. While some may provide us with a beautiful vista beyond the clouds of confusion and delusion, there may be others that lead us toward new clouds, ones on an unseen horizon, which still need to be seen and understood before we can hope to let in any amount of constant sunshine into our lives.

*

As we begin investigating our inner world and opening more fully to the full spectrum of our emotions, we may also find that it takes a while to feel comfortable within ourselves. Yet, just as a driver who practices in heavy traffic and treacherous conditions becomes skilled and confident, learning to anticipate the world that is speeding around him, secure in his ability to handle most difficult situations, so too is it with the practice of self-observation. As we become more familiar with our emotional traffic jams and stalls, we can begin to ever more accurately observe and decipher them. And just as a driver who has much experience knows when to speed up and when to slow down, when to yield and when to stop, we too can learn to anticipate and navigate the inner turmoil that is sure to arise from our own actions and our interactions with others.

As we continue exploring our inner world, we will begin seeing patterns within our life. We will discover similarities within many of our relationships and the circumstances we face. We will find ourselves questioning our automatic reactions to other people and begin wondering how we might act in ways that are less likely to hurt us and those around us. We may also begin to see how some of our reactions to certain situations are perhaps unwarranted or exaggerated and how they might be contributing to the pain we are experiencing. We may also discover that some of these behaviors are simply old patterns that are arising from reactions to past experiences we have judged as unpleasant. By investigating these moments when they occur, we can gain greater insight into how we might heal those old fears and hidden memories that are causing us to act in ways that often leave us feeling helpless, angry, and confused. We may also begin to see some of our own behaviors as wrong or immoral; actions that have brought us power, financial gain, or pleasure through the mistreatment of others.

All of these insights can be quite shocking and we may feel the urge to repress them again through continued numbing actions. Rather than running or hiding from your inner story, however, I would like to invite you to sit quietly, so that you might better understand how you are hurting yourself and how you might make changes that can help you.

And know that to enact any change effectively, we have to come from a place of truth. Be it an internal or external change, we must look as closely and as objectively as possible for any views arising from within that are tainted by fear or desire, and learn to look beyond them through eyes of truth.

*

As we begin to follow this path of being real with ourselves, of learning to explore and accept our fears and desires and trying to understand from where they have arisen, we will move toward greater clarity and understanding of ourselves and our world.

As we begin to see our lives with greater wisdom and compassion, we will begin to understand our own deepest desires and move toward the fulfillment of our true potential. Our lives will begin to move in more heartfelt directions and we will begin experiencing more happiness and inner peace. We will start to understand the connection that exists between us and with all things. And as we continue to heal ourselves, we will begin to clarify our stream of consciousness and dwell in greater harmony with the present moment and the world around us.

18

Understanding Our Thoughts

As we begin investigating our inner world, we will start to realize how abundant our thoughts actually are. We will see more clearly how they can lead us astray or overwhelm us with their intensity.

In those moments when we are feeling helpless or trapped by our thoughts and unable to do anything but suffer their burden, it is important to realize that they are not menacing villains bent on destroying our enjoyment of life, but actually very useful tools designed to help us better understand ourselves and recognize our true nature. Although it may seem as if they are harassing us, our thoughts are often trying to alert us to those feelings which we have not fully integrated. Like flags attached to sunken artifacts, they can point the way to our inner treasures - those precious parts of us that we have long hidden away or ignored.

*

Demanding or invasive thoughts often arise when we are unable to accept the emotions they represent. Instead of feeling the emotion and allowing it to pass through us, we resist it, and its energy and message persist in the form of thoughts. As we learn to see our thoughts in this way, we can begin moving our awareness away from them and back into our bodies, slowly becoming comfortable with even the most difficult emotions. In fact, when any thoughts do threaten to overpower us, it is important to follow their lead and "feel" the emotions that they are attached to. This is the best way to avoid spiraling into panic or obsession. By staying grounded in our bodies and feeling any sensations that are present, we can find a measure of control in even our most challenging moments. As we continue doing this, we will discover ways to change our perspectives and actions, and will slowly integrate all of our emotions. We will live more in the present moment and less "in our heads", moving from a state of constant thinking and worrying to one of simply being.

*

We also have to realize that it is impossible to escape our uncomfortable thoughts and emotions by simply focusing our attention on the outside world. We must, first and foremost, be present within ourselves. We cannot ignore ourselves and live in peace. Trying to "live in the moment" by forcing our attention on to the world around us is akin to holding an extremely heavy door open; we will succeed only until we become too tired to keep holding it. We will then have to run out of the way as it closes and will once again be trapped in an inner world of thought and sensation.

Rather than desperately forcing our awareness outward in the hopes of being present with life, we should instead look inward and direct our efforts toward taking the door of our own ignorance off of its massive hinges. By inspecting it carefully and learning how to loosen the rusty screws that keep it fastened to our own discomfort, we will slowly start to be more present. This takes a lot of patience and perseverance and we should be careful not to get frustrated when we are, time and again, locked up with only ourselves. If we can continue to soak the old screws of desire and pain in a solvent of our own love and compassion, however, we will begin opening to a world of greater peace in every moment.

19

The Key To True Happiness

As we begin to embrace our inner world with greater awareness, we will discover our constantly changing nature to be one of cause and effect and unmistakable impermanence. We will start to understand how our own actions influence the emotions we feel and also realize that we have a certain degree of control over our inner experience.

*

The sense of being a slave to our emotions can make us feel as if we are riding a crazed horse with no reins with which to control it. When we learn to let our bucking bronco writhe inside of us without jumping off at the nearest opportunity, however, we will more clearly begin to see how we have been contributing to our own discomfort by resisting our experience.

It is only by accepting any situation as it truly is and sitting with the feelings that it evokes in us that we can find true happiness. The next time you are feeling uncomfortable, try accepting your experience. Try saying to yourself, "I am aware that I am suffering." Then slowly and gently feel around for clues as to why you are in such a difficult place. By learning to observe ourselves in this way, we can begin to see any emotional turmoil within us as an opportunity to further understand and liberate ourselves from our unconscious fears and desires.

To admit that we are human and to have the dignity to acknowledge our fears and limitations is a very rare and courageous thing. With all of the unbalanced attention that our world gives to success, beauty, and material pleasure, this may actually be one of the most difficult things we might ever hope to do.

In many ways, we live in a world of denial - a world where weakness and fear are some of the biggest embarrassments imaginable. And rather than embrace the full spectrum of the human condition and the reality of whatever we might happen to be feeling, we instead typically strive for romantic, economic or social victories that might give us an illusion of control over our lives and our happiness.

By focusing only on our outer achievements, however, we can easily ignore the perfection that is within us and let ourselves be led astray from the healing power of our emotions and the wisdom of our inner world. We can also lose sight of the fact that we each possess unique creative gifts that can only be discovered by looking within us. These creative gifts hold the potential to fill us with a deep sense of purpose, confidence, and fulfillment. As we begin tapping into their energy, we will feel more empowered, engaged and alive for our spirits will be dancing to the tune of our own beat. We will also be of greater benefit to others for our unique gifts will no longer be hidden within us. We will finally be able to share who we truly are with the world and our authenticity and presence will be an inspiration to others.

And the key to finding this place – the key to finding our inner peace, power, and unique creative gifts – is one that we all possess. But, unfortunately, we have often been using it to open the wrong door.

For so long, we have been using this key - our own awareness - to open the door to judgment and comparison of ourselves with the world around us.

*

We tend to be keenly aware of those around us who are succeeding or failing and can easily lose our unique sense of self in our constant attempts to find our place within this hierarchy. We jump for joy when we succeed at our goals and become miserable when we fail. We often base our self-worth on how much we have or even how much we had in the past. "I used to be a great whatever" can become an almost invisible crutch to prop our sagging ego up with. Unfortunately, when we base our sense of happiness on our achievements, acquaintances, or acquisitions, we are setting ourselves up for disappointment; should these conditions somehow change in ways that we judge to be for the worse, we will likely discover our degree of happiness deteriorating as well.

*

We tend to forget our inherent wholeness in our never-ending search for happiness outside of us. Yet, how could we possibly ever feel like we are enough or that we have enough when we are constantly bombarded by advertisements for newer cars, thinner bodies, and more exciting lives? We are continuously lured into putting so much of our energy and attention into trying to improve our external world that we lose sight of the power and beauty of our inner one.

*

As we lose sight of ourselves in our computer and television screens, we also lose sight of the greater picture - of who we are and who we might become. We fail to see how we might live in ways that not only can help us become better people and better citizens of this planet, but that can reverse this dangerous, destructive trend we are currently on as a species. We are not separate from the earth and as we destroy her, we destroy ourselves. With every polluted river that is lost to unconscious manufacturing processes, we are one tiny bit less the people and the planet we potentially could be. By pretending that our actions have no consequence, we threaten ourselves and all species with further pain and suffering.

With a growing awareness of the effects of our actions on ourselves and those around us, however, we can make choices that result in greater connection and sustainability. And it is the same key that we have long used to judge others and ourselves that enables us to do this.

We have lost sight of the fact that this key, our own awareness, can also open a door that leads away from finding escape and freedom outside of us and, in fact, leads to true freedom - the freedom to be authentic, happy, and empowered. And to know our true creative gifts and be able to share them with the world.

*

As we start to realize that our previous attempts at filling ourselves up with things outside of us were, in fact, nothing more than hopeless attempts at concealing our inherent wholeness, we can begin to understand that we are, in this moment, already enough. And we can see that it is time to begin closing the door to our outer illusion and start putting this key into the door that leads to our inner world. And as we begin to open this door wider and wider to greater self-awareness and acceptance, we will start to realize that the path to true happiness is within us and that our previous attempts at finding fulfillment outside of us ultimately only led to more illusion and confusion.

*

By using our awareness to investigate our inner world instead of using it to judge our outer one, we will discover that we are capable of changing and growing in ways that will bring us more wisdom and inner peace.

And this is change not necessarily in terms of "self-improvement", where we are always striving to be more successful, wealthy, or beautiful, but in terms of "self-acceptance." And the difference between the two is vast. The former often leading us further and further from our true selves and closer to an idealized image which we hope will satisfy the critical analysis of those we are hoping to please. By attempting to gain praise, love, and approval from those around us, however, we can forget that by focusing on pleasing an external audience, we are working hard to make others happy, rather than ourselves. And, most importantly, we can miss out on the opportunity to discover the most important source of love we might ever hope to find: self-love.

20

One-night Stands

We tend to think that covering ourselves up with fancy clothes or expensive jewelry will make us feel more attractive and alive, and perhaps for a while it will - until the fashions change as they always do and we are left with a closet full of expensive clothes that we just couldn't possibly wear anymore.

As our purchases become outdated, however, we just might be able to notice our inner sense of self-worth fluctuate as well if we are watching carefully. We might discover that what we once longed for and were so proud of is now no longer enough, and as a result, we need something new to make us feel good.

*

"Oh, how these trends come and go. I can't believe I dressed like that!" we groan as we look at old photos taken of us.

Well, we should believe it. We should also believe that in twenty years the pictures taken of us today will probably look just as embarrassing. Or perhaps we will look back and long for how things were, forgetting how even at that time we may have been unconsciously trying to fit in with those around us (in our own unique way, of course).

"But wait," we might be thinking, "buying new things makes my life exciting. Without them my world would quickly become bland and boring!"

In order to discover true happiness and fulfillment, however, we need to look at our lives in a deeper light and realize that all pleasures found in outside attractions including food, sex, shopping, and sports are only temporary. Real fulfillment, real joy, can never be experienced while we are constantly engaged in the pursuit of pleasure and fun, of wealth and fame.

And yet, who among us doesn't want to be wealthy, famous, or powerful? Who, on some level, doesn't envy those men and women who seemingly have it all? So we continue to work and play hard, filling our days with attempts to satisfy our need for love and fulfillment.

*

We are constantly looking for more. More wealth, more toys, more fun. We want our one-night stands and can never seem to get enough. And these one-night stands are not just about sex; they can take many forms, some decidedly healthier than others. Charging from bar to bar and drink to drink is a common one-night stand. Another is a big ski day with some friends or staying up late watching too many episodes of that new tv series our co-worker told us about.

"But skiing or tv? How can they be bad for us? Sure, watching too much tv probably isn't the best thing to do, but skiing is most definitely a healthy activity. How could it possibly be considered a terrible "one-night stand"?"

To clarify, anything that is done solely to feel good can be considered a one-night stand because the satisfaction is only temporary.

Whenever we look for pleasure or base our self-esteem in activities outside of us, we will never be fulfilled or at peace. When we place our emphasis on our acquisitions or our achievements, we can easily lose touch with our true self, our true feelings, and the beauty that is found in every moment.

"But who cares?" we might say, "I am young (or young at heart) and having so much fun. What would there be to live for without exciting outlets like shopping, movies, and food? I get bored so easily and need my pleasures. If I was in a room all alone, I would go crazy."

Exactly. As long as we were looking for something to do or something to achieve or something to feel good about, we would become bored in a room all alone - or even a room full of fun things and people. We invariably tire of things when they fail to excite us and soon require stimulation from another source. We can see this in our own lives as we quickly become bored with our new clothes and gadgets, and need to have the latest and greatest thing on the market.

*

Always consuming and always wanting more, we are constantly looking for something that might satisfy the need within us for satisfaction and love. As we lose sight of ourselves in our designer sunglasses and our television screens, however, we fail to see how we are actually avoiding ourselves and destroying our home, the earth, with our unsustainable manufacturing practices and our insatiable desire to consume.

*

Our downfall as humans, be we from a wealthy or an aspiring land, is that we too often look for a sense of self and security from something which can never provide it. Constantly consuming, constantly needing more, we help convince each other that more is better and that less is never enough.

Our world is saturated with tempting one-night stands for pleasure seeking humans of all ages and nationalities. This isn't just a rich westerner's disease. It is especially prevalent in successful, wealthy nations, but is a plague just the same in poorer countries, hidden perhaps behind a tear that is the child of real hunger.

21

Healing Ourselves and Our World

With our attention constantly on things that will give us pleasure, we can easily forget that we are enough. We can also lose sight of the fact that as we take more and more from the world outside of us, we actually feel as though we have less and less. In this state of mind, our present belongings are never good enough and perhaps never fully enjoyed. We can also have difficulty finding contentment in our lives, especially when we are dealing with uncomfortable feelings or situations that aggravate us. As a result, we might long for a time when we will have no problems, when life will be easy. And, of course, when we compare our current life with its inherent and perfectly natural struggles and setbacks to some imagined life of perfection and ease (somewhere in the hopefully not too distant future) we can naturally feel even more dissatisfied. We can begin to regret any difficulties we may be facing and long for a future that might never arrive.

*

When we start to view our challenges as a way to grow in self-awareness and wisdom, however, we can begin to see our lives in a different light. The constant ups and downs that we experience can be seen as they truly are - the ebb and flow of life helping us progress on our spiritual journey.

*

We are constantly looking for ways to feel good. We resent life's struggles and our own limitations and are always trying to attain objects and experiences that will allow us to feel more pleasure. We are ruled by our minds and as a result are never satisfied.

*

We can easily find ourselves becoming bored with our lives and the things in it, although in reality it is not our environment which is boring. We often feel bored because we are failing to be enthralled by the beauty of the moment, by the mystery of even the smallest forms of creation. For example, are we able to stop and revel in the beauty of an ant on our picnic blanket or do we hurriedly brush it away, fearful of anything that might not fit into our picture of perfection?

*

As we begin viewing our lives with greater awareness, however, we will start to better understand the insatiability of our desires and the futility of our constant striving to have and be more.

We are constantly trying to make our lives more perfect, all the while failing to recognize the unfathomable perfection that they already are.

We often act as if we are in charge of life, becoming upset when someone or something defies our will. And yet, this often only leaves us feeling even more powerless. And, of course, we don't ever want to feel that way. We want to always feel strong and in control and right.

We lose sight every day of the beauty that surrounds us and the mystery that fills us. We often act as if we are adrift on an ocean of discontent, desperately clinging to whatever we can find that might give us pleasure or satisfaction. We avoid our fears and weaknesses, and constantly run from them toward things outside of us, always living as though we need more than we already have, than we already are.

*

As we begin accepting our smallness and our weakness, however, we can start to realize how limitless we truly are. As we begin letting go of our need for control and pleasure, we can start to see that we are, in fact, already okay. We can begin to understand how the act of accepting ourselves in every moment can free us from the need to look beyond ourselves for fulfillment. And we will find perhaps, simply by accepting and learning from all of our fears and desires, that we are more whole and more important than we ever thought possible. As we understand this, we can begin giving to ourselves instead of taking from others. We can start planting seeds of compassion within ourselves, instead of constantly engaging in a desperate search for outer fulfillment.

We can also begin to see how our need to grab onto pleasurable experiences that make us feel alive diminishes in direct proportion to our ability to accept whatever we are experiencing in any moment.

*

As we begin bringing a greater awareness to our fears and desires, we can start seeing our lives as an opportunity to grow in wisdom. Instead of spending our time constantly taking from the world to cover up our uncomfortable emotions, we can begin embracing them and learning from them. As we continue doing this, we will start to realize that life is supporting us in every way on our path to wholeness.

*

As we surrender our will to the hands of a greater power, we will in turn become empowered.

Instead of constantly running from ourselves in a never-ending pursuit of stimulating experiences, we can begin allowing everything to be exactly as it is.

And from this place of clarity and acceptance, we can learn to listen to our own heart and bravely follow it into action. We can begin improving our lives and our world by spreading love and presence. We can start to understand on ever-deeper levels that we are not only enough, but are tremendously powerful and capable of creating a life that is rich and fulfilling.

We can learn to work in harmony with nature and slowly stop acting like the world is our playground, as if we are superior to every other creature on this planet. As we do this, our long wounded inner children will learn to heal and play in peace, and we will begin to accept our roles as custodians for this world instead of always needing to be customers.

*

We can also, through our brave investigations into our own actions and behaviors, learn to see them in others. As we do this, a compassion will be bred that will enlighten the world. The constant threat of conflict that exists will eventually be transformed into an environment of acceptance and harmony.

*

Yet, perhaps we might think that this is an untouchable reality - one in which all humans are free, fed, and equal, and working together to create a world of peace. We can have difficulty imagining a world without borders or violence, a world where all men and women are brothers and sisters in the same family.

We have for so long led ourselves astray with our disparate beliefs that we have lost sight of the fact that we are all the same - perhaps from different countries and cultures - but the same nonetheless. We constantly judge each other on everything from our clothing to our political viewpoints and seem to feel justified in doing this simply because someone happens to be different than us. Yet is this really any different than how we treat everything in our world?

Aren't we just as quick to judge food or vacation spots as we are to judge people based on their nationality or appearance?

*

We are so quick to build walls and to defend them with our self-righteousness. We lose sight of the fact that we are all human beings and refuse, out of our own fear and insecurity, to accept those who are different from us. We often look down on those who don't measure up to our self-imposed standards, and in the process, slowly lose the desire to connect with them and accept them for who they truly are.

*

We can't seem to understand how our need to control our world so that we feel comfortable in it is destroying any hope of us actually doing that.

We have to remember that true peace is found in accepting reality and that running from ourselves and constantly passing judgment and hate onto those we feel different from is a very small way to live.

*

It is only by learning to accept our inner world and life as it is in any moment that we can discover true peace and freedom for ourselves and the world.

No government can eliminate the hate and greed within each of us. No outer body can make our individual and collective actions more mindful. The ability to realize our true potential can never be defined by a political agenda. We can never find true peace and understanding by simply enacting laws and regulations.

To heal ourselves requires great strength, patience, and perseverance.

To heal our world takes great individual healing.

*

The only way that our world will ever be at peace, with everyone happy and fulfilled, is if each of us, as individuals, begins taking responsibility for ourselves.

*

Yet, how can we ever possibly hope to do this if we, ourselves, are not healed? How can we expect others to stop killing and hating when we kill ourselves every day by abandoning those parts of us that we deem undesirable and hating those things that disturb us.

We run from our uncomfortable emotions at every turn and then criticize others for their selfish ways. Are we not just as selfish for needing to satisfy our lack of inner acceptance by constantly grasping at pleasures from the world around us?

*

The only way that we will ever heal ourselves is if we can own our feelings without running from them or acting them out. And, if we can learn to sit with ourselves without fighting the reality of our inner experience, we may be able to one day sit with our enemies instead of fighting with them.

*

We have to understand the importance of this. This is the only way to freedom and peace for each of us and our world.

*

It is up to each of us to free ourselves from the constant need to take from the world in order to fill ourselves up because we mistakenly think that we are not enough. Only we can see through the illusion that we are in some way lacking or deficient - that we need to have more to be more.

*

It is in the act of investigating and accepting all of the different elements that are within us that we can learn to see the truth and to find the courage to act upon it so that we can begin to heal ourselves and the world.

*

This is our true purpose in life and the path to true happiness and fulfillment.

To discover the world inside of us that is waiting to be explored and to lead us to our true self is the most beautiful, difficult, and important journey that any human being can engage in.

22

Discovering Our True Calling

So many of us are unhappy with our jobs and spend much of our time feeling burdened, bored, and unappreciated. We tend to view our daily grind as an obstacle that must be endured until we can eventually retire and be freed from our obligations to our employers and our lives of tedious responsibilities.

Until then, we tend to live for the weekend, when we can relax and revel in the freedom that our hard work has bought us. And we perhaps dream of one day retiring and purchasing a motor home or a vacation cabin on a lake - a place where we can lazily spend our remaining golden years in idle pursuit of our pleasures. We look forward to the day when we will finally being able to call all the shots, when we will have nothing to do except that which we want. A time when we will have no real responsibilities and no one to answer to.

Sounds nice, I suppose. Giving up our sense of "have to" for a comfortable sense of "want to". Finally reaching a state in our lives where all that we have to do is play and enjoy life as it was meant to be enjoyed. Ah yes, a life of relaxation and unlimited leisure. And un-fulfillment...

*

106

"What's that? Are you calling my well-deserved retirement unfulfilling? Are you insinuating that I am unhappy? My days are filled with tennis, golf, card games, and shopping. I am very busy and extremely fulfilled and wouldn't choose to live my life any other way!"

*

We are often quick to defend our right to our rewards and our pleasures, and this makes perfect sense. After all, aren't they what so often get us through our long days and our endless weeks? Aren't they what provide us with the hope and comfort that offset the burden of our never-ending responsibilities at work? Aren't they what make our lives more bearable? And, of course, there's nothing wrong with things like socializing, playing, and relaxing. They can help us find a more joyful and balanced life. But, unfortunately, if we are continuously resenting our time at work, they can even further compound the inherent craving and aversion that already exists within us. The pleasure and relief they provide can become disproportionately important to us and leave us feeling out of balance and constantly living for the future in the hopes of not having to accept the present.

*

But, of course, most of us must work. And we all want to feel as though we are worthwhile and contributing. We like to be inspired and challenged in our lives and our efforts. But are we? Do we feel engaged in ways that satisfy our inner creative longings? Or do we feel engaged to simply keep the threat of bills, poverty, and shame away?

Are we pursuing activities that fulfill us or are we simply valiantly working to support ourselves and our families, to keep the wheels in motion? Do we truly feel engaged or do we feel in some way resentful and reluctantly bound to our duties?

Do we rise every day with a deep hunger to fulfill our heart's desire, to walk our true creative path, or do we begrudgingly awaken to move one day closer to the weekend or to our retirement, when we can finally get our lives back?

Are we living life or are we living an obligation? Are we doing what totally fulfills us, whether we succeed or not? Whether we become famous or wealthy or not? Are we engaged in activities that feel pure and true to us? Ones that express who we are deep inside, that are authentically our own. Are we living an inspired life? A life where we taste an excitement born from doing rather than achieving. A life of connection and contentment. A life that challenges and rewards us for growing within ourselves. A life lived. A life fulfilled.

And if not, how might we?

"Well, let me see, what else can I do?" we say. "What job will give me back that sense of confidence and excitement that I felt when I was younger? What will make me feel happy and fulfilled?" And so we search through the want ads hoping to find our dream job.

*

Unfortunately, we forget that the only way we can truly find heart-felt work is by looking inward and following our heart, by listening to its gentle voice guiding us toward our true selves and our innermost creative gifts - our deepest callings. And in order to be able to hear this voice, we simply need to embrace our uncomfortable emotions and soothe their loud and lonely cries for attention.

But rather than doing this, we run from them and constantly look to our outer world to make us feel good and provide us with a false sense of fulfillment.

And so while we wait for our perfect job to appear, we end up looking for other ways to spice up our lives, to make them more exciting again.

"Maybe I should go on some more dates or get a new phone or binge watch that new series," we say. "Maybe I should go on a vacation or buy a nicer car or some new clothes."

*

We are always looking for ways to change our outer world so that we will feel better about ourselves and our lives, and often look for satisfaction in places that can only provide it temporarily such as new relationships, vacations, or clothing.

*

And what do we invariably find?

After a while, we realize that our new girlfriend or boyfriend isn't quite as perfect as we thought they were, our high tech devices have become outdated, and our clothes have gone out of style.

We begin to fall out of love. With ourselves and our lives.

*

And so we start searching again for that one thing or person that will satisfy us and make us feel whole so that we'll never have to feel bored or lonely again. And we keep wondering when we are going to get our chance, our lucky break. We envy those we know who have happened to find their "dream job", forgetting that the path to finding it is actually not outside of us, but within.

*

We have to realize that the only way we will ever find our dream job, our true calling - not to mention inner peace and fulfillment - is if we stop dreaming. If we wake up and look inward and embrace all of our uncomfortable emotions. And it is only after we have found the courage and taken the time to sit with them, to befriend them - to befriend ourselves – that we can access all of the power, stillness, and creativity that is within us, hidden below those very parts of us that we have long run from or tried to cover up. In many ways, these unwanted emotions are the gatekeepers to our inner kingdom and all of its beautiful treasures. In many ways, they hold the keys to our freedom.

23

God

Unless one has had a direct experience that allows them to relate to a power greater than themself, it can be really challenging to comprehend or even be open to the subject. As a result, many of us find it easier to simply leave God out of the equation and trust and believe only in ourselves. Maybe we see the world as a place to be conquered, as a competitive environment which we must face alone, with our success, not to mention survival, depending largely upon our ability to make astute decisions. As a result, the thought of assistance from a God that we have never seen or heard from can be difficult to accept. But perhaps a small part of us does still wonder "Is he real? Does he exist?"

*

Well, perhaps we would be better able to believe if we knew what to believe in. Is God simply a creation of the mind? Is he a supreme ruler, bringing down the law on those who are evil? (And if so, how come all of those corrupt businessmen and untouchable politicians are the ones living like kings?) Is he a compassionate soul who lets us get away with murder as long as we say we're sorry in a confessional? Or is he nothing? Just an old belief, sort of like Santa Claus. Someone who supposedly brings us gifts and joy, but like Ol' Saint Nick is never seen. Who are we to believe?

What is the truth?

*

The truth is that we want to feel empowered.

We don't like it when we're not in control or unable to solve problems. And since we can have trouble figuring out what God is all about, we can be tempted to just discard the whole concept out of hand and not even try to believe or figure it out. We can dismiss the idea of a higher power as just fantasy. Just stories.

Or maybe we do believe in God. Maybe we do think that all of those stories about him that have been passed down throughout the ages are true. Stories from a simpler time, maybe hundreds, if not thousands of years ago, when men somehow knew God. But what if the religious leaders who told us these stories were misinformed? What if they were only offering us arcane and dogmatic versions of ancient beliefs and rituals that failed to reflect any true understanding of God, spirituality, or our own inherent divinity? What if their teachings were simply well-meaning, but inherently limited attempts to quantify and compartmentalize God so that we might in some way be able to rationalize and relate to him? For example, it is perhaps easier for us to imagine God as a human-like creature, not unlike ourselves in appearance, but with unlimited, unseen, and not fully understood powers. But perhaps we say that God made us in his image so that we feel comfortable when thinking about Him. As if he is some gentle, old caretaker with a garden full of little incarnations of Himself running around (only who are smaller and not quite as smart...). Perhaps the truth, however, is that we have created him in our image, rather than the other way around. This would seem natural considering the fact that many of us believe we are the superior being in God's garden. That all other creatures have simply been dispensed for our own needs. As if the lakes and the birds and the trees were made for us to do with as we desire. That we are more "God-like" than any other creature... And maybe we also like to imagine God as some sort of male carpenter figure who worked his butt off for six hard days and kicked back in the sun on Sunday to enjoy "his" handiwork. But do we actually believe God works according to our seven-day week? Or that he needs a day to recuperate from all of his creating?

*

Perhaps we have taken these leader's beliefs on faith, not considering for a second that we, too, are the righteous children of God. That we, too, are her creations and that as such we have every right to discover her power and beauty. Yes, her.

Why, after all, is God considered to be a man? Why, if women are the mothering spirits, the "givers of life", wouldn't God be "classified" as a woman? (Are we able to see how referring to God as a "he" disempowers women and is a reflection of a past full of injustices and inequities against them by the church and state? Can we understand how this type of patriarchal definition provides insight into our society's tendency to empower men and make them the gatekeepers of all that is sacred?)

*

When we look for definitions of God we are ultimately searching for a sense of sureness and safety within ourselves. We are most afraid of the unknown, so we try to compartmentalize God and say that we know what he wants, but really we are saying that we know what we want.

We try to bring God down to size so that we can feel comfortable and secure in our beliefs.

But what exactly do we believe?

Do we believe in the perfection of life or are we constantly praying to God to show us the way to a better one? Do we think that God helps us only when we ask her to? Have we considered that maybe the answers we are seeking are right under our nose, being presented to us in every moment? Perhaps our prayers might instead be seen as an opportunity to open to the Divine presence that is already within us and around us, constantly guiding our lives so that we can better understand and empower ourselves.

Maybe we should be praying to hear God rather than the other way around.

*

Perhaps we fear ourselves and our discomfort and want God to make everything better so that we don't have to accept the reality of our life. Maybe we think that God is only about happiness, pleasure, and success. That our fears are not a part of us or a part of God. That God is all sunshine and bright skies. That "God's country" is only in the Rocky Mountains or some other beautiful place.

*

Have we considered that God might be speaking to us through our discomfort? That she might be communicating with us through our every experience? Have we forgotten that God is in charge and that we can never run from our discomfort; that she will help us to feel it through the emergence of similar situations over and over again until we accept and learn from them?

*

It is important to understand that nothing is inherently bad - even our uncomfortable emotions and experiences. We call things bad that we don't like, if they make us feel uncomfortable inside. We complain about the people and the situations in our lives, failing to consider that they might be exactly what we need for our spiritual growth. We tend to resist these opportunities to learn about ourselves, however, and often run from them toward situations that will hopefully make us feel good and provide us with a false sense of power.

*

We have to realize that every event, no matter how uncomfortable or seemingly insignificant, has meaning and purpose. We need to understand that every moment is an opportunity to grow in wisdom, acceptance, and inner peace. Yet, we are so afraid of failure, pain, and discomfort that we often cannot see the beauty in them or acknowledge their Divine presence in our lives.

The more that we can begin accepting these uncomfortable experiences as they come into our lives, however, the more we can begin opening up to the perfection of life, the perfection of God, the perfection that we are - in every moment.

*

God is not separate from life. God is life.

God is the snow falling, the child playing, the leaves turning brown in the autumn wind. God is the night sky, full of stars, and the daybreak, full of life. God is our success and our failure. Our happiness and our sadness. God is both the love that we feel and the uncomfortable relationships we are in, constantly urging us on to know ourselves and to change in ways that feel right, in ways that reveal our true strength, our true worth, and our true purpose.

God is in every moment and every event - even the "bad" ones.

God is in everything. And everything is God.

24

Knowing Ourselves

Every time that we face our fears, we move one step closer to ourselves. As we bravely confront and act upon our inner truths, we prove to ourselves that our voice matters and that we can trust ourselves.

It is in this trusting that our true confidence emerges.

*

It is infinitely more empowering to boldly acknowledge our fears and weaknesses than to pretend they don't exist. When we choose reality, such as the reality of our fear, we can start learning from and integrating all of our emotions and emerge as stronger, more whole individuals.

*

We often think that we need to achieve some external success before we can be happy or fulfilled, but the truth is that no accomplishment can compare to the power and peace that we can reclaim by accepting all of our emotions.

*

As we start investigating our inner world, we will begin to notice that when we focus solely on outer pursuits, our egos tend to inflate and deflate as our successes come and go. When life is good and things are going our way, we typically feel happy and free. When things aren't working out, however, our spirits tend to sag and our confidence deflates. Rather than taking the time to acknowledge our uncomfortable emotions and the wisdom they contain, however, we tend to keep striving to reach the goals we have laid out for ourselves. And while there is nothing wrong, of course, with setting goals and working to attain them, we often overlook the lessons that life and our setbacks are trying to teach us; lessons that might help us even more clearly recognize our true path and purpose.

*

We often lose sight of our own humanness in an attempt to be more than human. Weakness, anger, and fear, and the insights they can provide are profoundly undervalued in our society and the world at large. We are so prone to want to run from or cover up our scary emotions when we suffer a loss or disappointment in our lives. If we look closely, however, it is often our greatest gift to meet with failure or be exposed in some painful way. To have to truly face our own vulnerability and embrace our fears is an opportunity to discover the most important type of knowledge we might ever hope to attain – self-knowledge.

And we are all given the opportunity to learn from life and to grow within ourselves in these ways. No one can hide this or take it from us. The strength, wisdom, and self-love that this type of self-inquiry can generate can't be bought in any store or received from anyone else. The only place that we can find it is within ourselves.

*

As we continue exploring our inner world and digesting our own illusions, a clarity will emerge from within and we will be drawn closer and closer to our true path. We will lose sight of the distractions of our past and will begin to see our previous accomplishments perhaps more as preparations for this inner journey than as victories unto themselves.

We will also automatically learn to embrace change, to depend on it as we do our breath. Change will become the gasoline for the truth seeking vehicle that we are.

We will also find, perhaps, that unless we continue to walk through the valleys and seemingly endless mountain peaks of our inner fears and desires, we will hear our soul cry. For once tasted, freedom becomes a goal unto itself. A mission for life and a reason to live.

*

As we keep progressing on our inner path, we may also begin to realize how foolish we have been - how egotistical and afraid and unable to acknowledge it. As we continue accepting and integrating all of our emotions, however, we will start to remove our disguises and emerge as unique individuals who are less affected by society's influences. Yet, we may conversely also feel more a part of our world than ever and see more clearly how we can help heal it.

We will also begin to more clearly realize, in ways that we can never hope to fully explain or understand, how all of our experiences and interactions are perfectly designed opportunities to help us grow in awareness.

We will also start to more deeply appreciate the majesty of our existence and the beauty of our world. And we will more clearly understand our purpose in life and in the lives of others.

*

We will also start to finally realize that we are enough and will recognize all of the trappings of society that we have long used to hide from ourselves as simply vain attempts to control something that is, in fact, controlling us: life.

*

Many of us have seemingly forgotten how to be at peace with ourselves and others, and unless we choose to turn our hungry minds inward, we will remain in an uncomfortable state of longing for the acceptance and love that ultimately only we can provide ourselves.

*

We have to begin embracing all of our emotions and start finding the courage to listen to our hearts so that we can effect change in truthful directions.

This is our moral responsibility to ourselves and our world.

This is change not for "change's sake", but for the need to breathe clean air into our polluted bodies and minds.

This is a quest for the truth so that we might once again be free of the need to please and the need to hate.

This is about living a life fulfilled because we have chosen to be lived by life.

This is about not controlling life, but learning to let it guide us and teach us. To help us, not hurt us.

*

Only we can hurt ourselves by remaining in resistance and discomfort.

Only we can unconsciously stay in reaction mode, letting life and other people push us and pull us like puppets on strings.

*

By not letting ourselves feel our fears and accept our weaknesses, we become like rigid oil platforms, unable to withstand the torrential storms of life. Desperately grasping for crude forms of pleasure, we fail to see the real source of richness that lies deep within us.

*

We seem to think that pretending we're not scared will keep us strong. We forget, however, that acknowledging our inner storms is what enables us to let more sunshine into our lives. When we can admit that we are fearful at times, we can begin to find our true strength. If we're unwilling to do this, however, and continue to stand unyielding against the inevitable inner storms of life, we will miss out on the lessons they are trying to provide us and continually get a little more blown off course, slowly being swept ever deeper into a world of false dreams and imagined satisfaction. And as a result, we can forget where we came from and lose sight of our inner compass that can get us safely back home.

Yet even as we do begin acknowledging the reality of our emotions and start making our way back home to a place of greater inner peace, fulfillment, and connection with ourselves, it is important to remember that this return journey will not always be easy.

Yes, it will get easier, eventually, but for a long time you may feel more confused and alone than ever. No longer safe in the mirage of your dreams, slowly awakening to the reality of your inner world, you may suddenly begin to wish that you had never taken that first look inside. That you had never prayed to God to show you the truth. That you had never read this book.

But please trust that by acknowledging and bringing attention to your inner pain, your wounds will eventually heal. Yet, just as a child would rather go play outside with their friends than admit they were sick, we have to be aware of our mind's desire to lead us once again off of our true course and back to the land of imagined fulfillment outside of us. We need to remain strong and have faith that our wounds will heal. And to heal them, we must give constant and daily attention to them, soothing them with our love, patience, and acceptance.

*

It is important to understand that this inner journey is one which never truly ends, although it does become easier the more that we continue on it. And as we begin this journey back into ourselves, we will discover that the path to freedom is lit with candles of truth and flames of exuberance from within.

*

This process of self-realization takes a while to get the hang of, but once we become adept at experiencing an outside event and then looking inward to determine what we are feeling and why we are feeling it, we will become proficient at responding to life and all of its lessons with greater wisdom, acceptance, and patience. As we continue to search for our personal truths and embrace our deepest fears and desires, we will move toward greater inner peace and clarity.

*

As we begin living with greater self-awareness, our lives will be filled with a deeper sense of purpose and accomplishment. We will start to experience more gratitude and will focus less on what we don't have and more on what we do.

We will also begin to understand why this inner journey is the most important and difficult undertaking that any human being can attempt.

*

Whenever we try to cover up our uncomfortable emotions by acting overly positive, we are, on some level, ignoring reality and losing an opportunity to connect more deeply with ourselves and with life. This disconnect will continue until we can begin accepting all of our experiences and those very things that can make us more whole: our weakness, fear, and pain. It is much more foolhardy to say, "I am okay" when we actually aren't than it is to look within and admit that we are hurting in ways that we perhaps do not want to acknowledge.

*

When we choose the reality of a situation over how we would prefer it to be, we take bold steps toward embracing life on its own terms. As we start to accept our experience in any moment, be it something we would have previously labeled "good" or something we would have labeled "bad", we can begin to more fully accept ourselves as well.

*

Often we are led into areas of personal weakness so that we can ultimately emerge more whole, with a greater degree of acceptance and trust of ourselves and life.

We are presented with challenges so that we can face them with our inner light of truth and emerge stronger, wiser, and more at peace.

If life were easy, we would be so small. It is the mountains that we must climb that strengthen us.

It is looking within ourselves and following our inner compass that teaches us to trust ourselves and our instincts.

And to trust that God is always with us, always watching and encouraging us on in our struggle to be whole.

In our struggle for self-acceptance, peace, and empowerment.

*

And yet, why is God doing this?

Why is she doing everything at all times to keep us on an ever-broadening path of truth and awareness? Why is she helping us?

*

As we begin exploring our inner world, we will begin to realize that God is providing us with all of our experiences so that we can accept and learn from them, and heal ourselves and grow in self-awareness and wisdom. So that we can become ever more insightful, compassionate, and empowered individuals with a clearer sense of who we truly are and how we might express our unique gifts to the world.

Once we begin investigating our inner world and trusting our inner voice, we can start following it and allow our inner compass to lead us in directions that feel more heartfelt. If we are not able to access our inner compass, however, we might find ourselves off-track, following footsteps that are not necessarily ours to follow.

For example, let's say your dad, your grandpa, and your great-grandpa were all lawyers and since you were knee-high, you have been subtly (or maybe not so subtly) urged to follow in their paths. If you didn't know any better (i.e. if you didn't know yourself), you might just follow their lead and go on to become a lawyer without ever questioning the validity of your decision. Or maybe you would do anything else just to spite them and show them that you weren't going to be like them. What it really comes down to, though, is that the only way to know whether you are truly a lawyer at heart is to know your own heart.

*

You see, the whole purpose of this "know yourself" thing is for you to know yourself.

It is kind of like this - if a horse thought it was a cow because its uncle, dad, and brothers thought that they were cows, Ol'

McDonald would have a pretty mixed up farm, wouldn't he? Well, God is sort of like Ol' McDonald and she wants her farm in order. She wants her horses neighing, her ducks quacking, and her cows mooing. And she wants her singers singing, her writers writing, her painters painting, and her healers healing. And the only way that she is ever going to get that is if we all figure out our parts.

*

When we see someone that flows at what they do, that is a "natural", we are all in awe of their talents.

Well, the truth is that we are all "naturals", but perhaps we aren't exactly sure at what. We all have the potential to share our personal gifts with the world, but perhaps we aren't even quite sure what they are.

And yet, we wonder how we end up in jobs that leave us bored and uninspired. And we begin to hate our life and all of its drudgery. The spark is gone and we're out of gas. And we're only in our forties. Or maybe even our twenties!

"How did I get so side-tracked?" we wonder. "Why do I feel so hopelessly lost?"

*

Well, perhaps we might consider that we've never even truly had our eyes open.

Perhaps we have mistaken our achievements and our acquisitions for who we thought we really were and are just now beginning to realize that we are a whole lot more.

Perhaps we are ready to wake up to our inner reality and to our potential as unique individuals.

Perhaps we are ready to stop dreaming and to start living.

To let life guide us back to ourselves and a more authentic and fulfilling life.

In this and every moment.

25

Summary

The truth is a very powerful element in our lives if we allow it to be.

It is our key to a constantly evolving sense of self-respect and freedom.

It is an anchor, a sail, and a life preserver on the seas of deception and enticement.

With truth we are strong and free. Without it we are in a state of constant confusion.

*

To know ourselves, we have to befriend the truth.

To be fully alive, we must learn to look for it in every moment.

*

Every experience, regardless of its content, is a perfectly designed opportunity for us to understand and accept deeper truths about ourselves. As we begin embracing these insights, we can start to extricate ourselves from the self-limiting, unconscious behaviors that have kept us small, afraid, and separate from ourselves and from life.

*

As we begin embracing our inner reality, we will grow in awareness and equanimity. We will begin associating ourselves with "the watcher", that part of us that is of unlimited depth and compassion. That part of us that is able to observe our fears and desires rising up and, instead of helplessly reacting to them with no profitable aim, use them as a way to grow in wisdom and compassion.

*

As we begin observing ourselves, we will start to see that there are many things that we are not in control of. And as we grow in acceptance of those things that we can't change, we will become empowered to make constructive changes wherever and whenever we can. No longer finding ourselves saying, "Why me?" or "How did I get here?", we will understand that life is providing us with exactly what we need in every moment to help us grow in insight and awareness, no matter how challenging that may be.

And yet this can be one of the more difficult aspects of this inner path; to realize how truly painful and confusing our lives may be can make us long for the chance to start from an easier place with a view unobstructed by so many weeds of irresponsibility and ignorance. Yet, our place to begin this journey into acceptance and growth, into owning ourselves and our lives once again, must begin in this very moment, no matter how difficult that might seem.

And so, as we dare to take that first step, or that thousandth, we need to know that we are not alone on this path. We have to remember that life is holding us in her bosom, providing us with all of the tools that we need to realize our potential in every moment.

*

This life is ours and is for us.

We are so valuable and precious, that God and her universe are doing everything possible for us at all times, whether we realize it or not, to help us come to know ourselves and our true gifts so that we can help them be born into the world.

*

We can stand around all day, all year, or our whole lives, saying, "What should I do with my life?", but unless we are willing to undertake that long, painful, most beautiful voyage back into our own hearts, this question will forever be left unanswered.

*

With every fear or painful encounter, life is trying to harvest us so that we can fill its basket with our own personal fruit. So that we can better understand ourselves and accept and learn from all of our emotions and grow into individuals who are open to the music of the heavens moving through them. So that we can become a vehicle for the perfection of life; a unique instrument being played as only we can. So that we can sing the song that wants to move through us. The song that only we can tune into. That only we can hear.

*

As we begin looking for the truth within us and start acting upon it, our ability to resonate with it improves. We start to become more authentically creative and move into a place of doing - not for taking from life, but for giving back to it.

*

As we begin integrating all of the elements within us, we will become less and less buffeted by the winds of change and instead start looking to them as indicators of where our vessel should head. We will learn to leave the false security of our contrived harbor of fear and desire and head out on to the sea of possibility, knowing that an eternally safe and secure port exists within us at all times.

*

As we learn to run not to outer comforts when we feel upset, but to ourselves, we will find a strength forming that is born not of struggle, but of acceptance. A strength built upon a constant turning to our inner world and our own needs.

*

Our own attention and compassion are such powerfully healing things.

It is important for us to realize this and to begin turning our awareness not so much to the world around us, but to the ways in which we react to avoid the discomfort within us.

*

To be whole means to accept ourselves as we are. To learn to see our weaknesses and our fears as no better and no worse than any other part of us.

As our acceptance of these and all of the other elements within us increases, we will lose sight of the temptations that for so long have brought us comfort and instead find salvation in the simple act of holding our own hand, as it has always been held by the universe, down that long and often dark path that we call ourselves.

For every time that is taken.

For every love that is lost.

For every moment that we feel small, confused, and afraid, we are enough.

With our hopes and our fears, our dreams and our disappointments, our loves and our hates, our lives and our deaths.

With each and every step that we take, know that God is by our side and that she hears our calls.

That she hears our small voices in the dark and stormy night.

Calling out to her and to ourselves for truth, peace and love.

Now and always.

About the Author

Geoff Bell-Devaney has been practicing and teaching mindfulness for over twenty years and is a former resident of the Kripalu Center for Yoga and Health and a 2001 graduate of the Mindfulness-Based Stress Reduction Teacher Training program at the Center for Mindfulness at the UMass Medical School. He is also the author of *A Mindful Approach To Parenting: Insights on Raising Our Children With Wisdom, Awareness, and Acceptance.*

The audio version of this book, videos, and more can be found at:

www.geoffbell-devaney.com

www.ingramcontent.com/pod-product-compliance
Lightning Source LLC
LaVergne TN
LVHW041320080426
835513LV00008B/529